KIDS' GUIDE TO EXPLORING THE BIBLE

A. L. Rogers

KIDS' GUIDE TO EXPLORING THE BIBLE

Tools, Techniques, & Tips for Digging into God's Word

BARBOUR **kidz**

A Division of Barbour Publishing

Print ISBN 978-1-64352-997-4

The author is represented by the literary agency of Credo Communications, LLC, Grand Rapids, Michigan, credocommunications.net.

Published by Barbour Publishing, Inc., 1810 Barbour Drive, Uhrichsville, Ohio 44683, www.barbourbooks.com

Our mission is to inspire the world with the life-changing message of the Bible.

Member of the
Evangelical Christian
Publishers Association

Printed in China.

000804 0821 RP

TO
MAURICE, KIRSTEN,
BIANCA, AND SHAY

CONTENTS

INTRODUCTION

The Most Gigantic Book You've Ever Read

What's the most gigantic book you've ever read? Was it a seven-book series filled with action and adventure? Was it a book with a million chapters? Was it the dictionary? (Or, if you don't read that much, was it a comic book? The back of a cereal box?)

Whether you love to read or not, we can all agree that big books are intimidating! Page after page and chapter after chapter of a giant book with no pictures can be a snooze-fest.

But that can raise a problem. As Christians, we should read and study the Bible—the most gigantic book of them all! But why? It was written like a bazillion years ago. Why read it now?

In this book we're going on an expedition to answer those questions. This book is way shorter than the Bible, so it won't be a long journey. (Whew!) But it might just change your life. Inside the Bible are the words of God, telling you how much He loves you. Reading the Bible is an amazing way to grow closer to Him.

On this journey, you'll find out what the Bible is, what's inside it, and how to read—and even enjoy—it. Even better, you'll learn how to take God's wisdom in the Bible and put it to good use in your life.

Those are our goals for the journey. You'll learn:

- Why we read the Bible

- What the Bible is

- What's inside the Bible

- How to apply it to your life

Read on, adventurers! The Bible might be big and intimidating, but we will tackle it together. (Plus, there are lots of pictures and fun stuff in this book, so it won't be a snooze-fest!)

Unless otherwise noted, all Bible quotations are taken from the New Life Version of the Bible.

CHAPTER ONE

The Greatest Commandments in the Universe (Why We Read the Bible)

A proud religious law-keeper who knew the Law tried to trap Jesus. He said, "Teacher, which one is the greatest of the Laws?"
MATTHEW 22:35–36

Rules. Are they fun? Not really. But rules are often meant to keep people safe, healthy, and happy. "Don't run with scissors" will keep you from a painful accident. "Wash your hands before you eat" will get rid of germs and prevent you from getting a cold. "Never mix orange juice and milk" is just plain genius. (Who would do that anyway? Yuck!)

Some rules are so important they are called *commandments*—rules that simply *must* be followed. "Don't tell lies" is a good example.

But which rules are the greatest? I'm glad you asked!

Jesus was asked this same question. He said the greatest commandment is to "love the Lord your God with all your heart and with all your soul and with all your mind." But He didn't stop with just one. The second greatest commandment, Jesus said, is like the first: "You must love your neighbor as you love yourself."[1]

There you have it. The most important rules in the whole universe are to *love God* and *love others*. Sounds easy enough.

But wait! If that's all we have to do, why do we need to read the Bible at all?

Great question! Just like a scientist digging up dinosaur bones, let's dig up some answers. Grab your shovels! Grab your hard hats! This caravan is moving out!

WHY WE NEED TO READ THE BIBLE

Just like cookies and cream, the two main reasons for reading the Bible cannot be separated:

1) To know God

2) To grow in wisdom

Know and *grow*.

KEY WORD

Commandment

A *commandment* is an important rule that must be followed. There are a few commandments in the Bible. Some of the most famous are called "The Ten Commandments," which God gave to the nation of Israel. That story is found in Exodus 20:3–17.

These commandments were extremely important. But, rather than seeing them as God's rules for protection, some Jewish law-teachers (from groups called Pharisees or Sadducees) used them to control people. The Jewish teacher who asked Jesus about the greatest commandment wanted to trap Him. Would Jesus dare say that one commandment is better than the rest?

Jesus was smarter than that. He pointed out that the whole law of God could be summed up in two commandments: love God and love others. The man was speechless!

God doesn't make rules to control us or take away our fun. His rules guide us into happier lives. Just like the rules in soccer ("no hands!") make the game more fun and the rules of the road ("buckle up!") keep us safe, God's commandments show us how to live with freedom and joy.

Now you might be thinking, "Wait a minute. Didn't Jesus say the two greatest commandments are to love God and love others? It's easy to see how 'knowing God' helps us love Him—when we know who He is and what He desires the most, our love for Him just comes naturally. But can growing in wisdom help us love others?"

Once again, great question!

The answer is yes! Growing in wisdom is one of the best ways to learn how to love others.

*You have known the Holy Writings since you were a child. **They are able to give you wisdom** that leads to being saved from the punishment of sin by putting your trust in Christ Jesus.*

2 TIMOTHY 3:15

Wisdom is the ability to make choices that please God.[2] It's a combination of knowledge and experience. Sometimes, just *knowing* something doesn't mean much unless you've had some hands-on *experience* too.

For example, imagine that someone tells you, "Whenever it is cold outside, wear a jacket." You know that rule by heart. But one cold day you leave the house in a hurry, forgetting your jacket. The world feels like a giant refrigerator all day long! Weeks later, your friend invites you to go bike riding. You're not sure if the weather will be warm or cold, so you grab your jacket. Better safe than sorry!

That is wisdom. What you knew and what you experienced helped you make a good decision.

The whole book of Proverbs is about wisdom. In the second chapter, we learn that "the Lord gives wisdom. Much learning and understanding come from His mouth" (Proverbs 2:6). In the next chapter, the author writes, "My son, do not forget my teaching. Let your heart keep my words. For they will add to you many days and years of life and peace. Do not let kindness and truth leave you. Tie them around your neck. Write them upon your heart. So you will find favor and good understanding in the eyes of God and man" (Proverbs 3:1–4).

In Bible times, these instructions were often taught to children just like you. Jesus Himself taught kids about God's wisdom, even when His disciples tried to shoo them away (Matthew 19:13–15).

Sometimes love comes easy. For example, it's easy to say, "I love you!" when your mom (or another grown-up who cares about you) surprises you with ice cream. But what about when it's hard? How should you treat someone who is always gone, grumpy, or making bad choices that hurt you? In these situations, only wisdom can help you keep Jesus' second commandment. By knowing God and gaining His wisdom from the Bible, you'll never run out of "kindness and truth." You will "find favor and good understanding" with God and others.

GROWING IN WISDOM AND BURIED BONES

Do you know what the biggest bone in your body is? It's your femur—the bone that stretches inside your thigh from your knee to your hip.

Here's another cool science question: What was the first dinosaur bone ever discovered? You guessed it—a femur! In 1676 in Oxfordshire, England, a big chunk of bone was found encased in limestone. Scientists later identified it as part of a giant lizard creature, which they named *Megalosaurus*. Eventually this lizard creature—and others like it—would come to be known as dinosaurs!

This discovery launched a whole new branch of science called *paleontology*. Paleontologists are the people who study the fossils of dinosaurs and prehistoric creatures.

There's also a similar branch of science, *archaeology*, that focuses on artifacts—evidence of human life and culture that is buried deep in the earth.

Over the centuries, paleontologists and archaeologists have discovered thousands of fossils and artifacts.

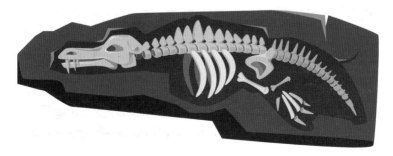

Discoveries such as the size of a pterodactyl's wing, the height of a Tyrannosaurus rex, or the way ancient Egyptians buried their mummies have completely changed our understanding of God's creation and the people who first lived in it. They give us glimpses into the past and inspire us with possibilities of the future.

That's what studying the Bible is like! The deeper you "dig" into the Bible, the more treasures you'll discover—just like an archaeologist finding a rare coin from an ancient civilization. It will completely change your life.

The first step is knowing God. Let's look at three ways to do that.

THREE WAYS TO KNOW GOD

There are three ways we can learn about God:

1) Through creation (the natural world)

2) Through the Bible

3) Through Jesus

Since exploring the Bible is what this book is all about, we're going to spend a lot of time on #2. But for now, let's look at all three of them together for a full picture of who God is.

1) CREATION

We can learn things about God by studying His creation. Psalm 19:1-3 says, "The heavens are telling of the greatness of God and the great open spaces above show the work of His hands. Day to day they speak. And night to night they show much learning. There is no speaking and no words where their voice is not heard." Later, Romans 1:20 says, "Men cannot say they do not know about God. From the beginning of the world, men could see what God is like through the things He has made. This shows His power that lasts forever. It shows that He is God."

This book is about studying the Bible, so we won't be able to spend much time on creation. But it's a great idea to study nature on your own. Animals, plants, stars, planets, the human body and brain all show us how creative and powerful God is.

For example, think about all the details that make the earth a perfect place for us to live: the tilt of the earth on its axis (about 23.5 degrees), the distance from the earth to the sun (about 92.5 million miles), the moon's orbit and its effect on the tide, and a thousand other details. If just one of these were off by a hair, the whole planet would change. Yet these details combine to make earth safe for humans, animals, and plants. According to the Bible, this is the work of God.

So pay close attention in science class and study the world around you! All creation reveals God's intelligence, creativity, and love for life.

2) THE BIBLE

Imagine sitting at the kitchen table with your grandma. You're about to go on your next paleontology trip to discover the bones of some amazing new dinosaur. (Maybe you'll name it the *Amazing-a-saurus*! Or something bigger, like the *Giganto-Huge-Amazing-a-saurus*.)

Back to the kitchen table with Grandma. As she puts a plate of warm cookies on the table, delicious smells fill the air. Yum! She sits down across the table and smiles.

Suddenly, it hits you—there are so many things you've always wanted to know about your grandma, and this is your chance to ask! Questions jump in your mind like popcorn, springing from the same curiosity that fuels your hunt for dinosaur bones:

- What was it like when you were my age?
- Who was your best friend?
- What was your favorite movie?
- What's the best birthday gift you've ever gotten?
- What's the funniest joke you know?

Sit down with your grandma (or an important older lady in your life) and have a conversation like this sometime. What makes her laugh? What makes her sad? Find out what things are most important to her, and ask her to tell you stories about her life. Ask her anything you can think of.

You will be amazed by what you learn! Grandmas (and older people in general) have a lot of good stories to tell. In fact, it will probably take more than one conversation to really get to know her. She has lived a long time and has a lot to share! You will also feel loved as she spends time telling you about herself.

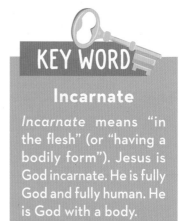

KEY WORD

Incarnate

Incarnate means "in the flesh" (or "having a bodily form"). Jesus is God incarnate. He is fully God and fully human. He is God with a body.

The same is true with God. Even though we can't see God sitting in a chair in our kitchen, we *can* read His Word, the Bible. That's how God speaks to us. When we read it, we get to know Him by learning what He is like. We learn how God acts, what He thinks, what's important to Him, and what brings Him joy and sadness. Even better, we learn what He has done to show us His love. The Bible *reveals* who God is.

The Triune God

Does it seem weird that both Jesus and the Father are God? How can Jesus be fully God and fully human at the same time? Does it feel like your head is going to explode?

Christians have believed (and wrestled with) these mysterious ideas for centuries. The Bible teaches that God is *triune*—meaning He is three separate persons and one God at the same time.

The third person? That would be God's Spirit, often called "the Holy Spirit." All three persons are fully God. He is three in one, or triune.

Does this seem hard to understand? Don't worry. Even though it's a good idea to pray for understanding and talk about "the Trinity" with your parents or church leaders, you don't need to completely understand it to love God or read His Word. God is powerful, wise, and far beyond human understanding, making it hard for us to describe Him sometimes. It also makes focusing on Jesus—who is God in the flesh—that much more important.

3) JESUS

Christians believe that Jesus is God *incarnate*. This word means "in the flesh." Throughout the Bible, Jesus is called both "the Son of Man" and "the Son of God" (Mark 2:10; Luke 1:30-32). In other words, He is both God and human at the same time. Jesus once said, "I am the Way and the Truth and the Life. No one can go to the Father [God] except by Me" (John 14:6). He also said, "My Father [God] and I are one!" (John 10:30).

Jesus said these things about Himself to help us understand what "God incarnate" means: *Jesus is God*. He and God (often called "the Father") are different persons, but they are the same God. This means that if we want to know God—to understand what's important to Him, what He thinks is bad, and how He acts—then we should pay close attention to Jesus. He is God in the flesh.

TIME TO REVIEW!

In Matthew 22:36–40, Jesus gives us two commandments that sum up all of God's Word. What are they?

1) Love the _Lord_ your _God_ with all your _heart_, and with all your _soul_ and with all your _mind_ .

2) Love your _neihter_ as you love yourself.

There are two main reasons for reading the Bible: to *know* and *grow*. These two things will help us keep Jesus' greatest commandments.

Who do we want to know? What do we want to grow in?

There are three ways to know God:

1) Through creation
2) Through the Bible
3) Through Jesus

CHAPTER TWO

Prepare for Travel (Getting Ready to Spend Time with God)

Never stop praying.
1 THESSALONIANS 5:17

Archaeologists begin their work long before they set out on the road. They spend months, sometimes years, figuring out where to dig. These studies are called *surveys*. During this time, archaeologists study maps, history, and other pieces of information to find the locations with the most buried artifacts.

Some trips take them to the freezing tundra of Antarctica! Others to the flaming hot sands of the Sahara Desert!

But these journeys aren't free. Before they can go anywhere, archaeologists must raise money and buy the right equipment for their dig. Some also take a team—who may require training—along with them.

In short, archaeological digs require a lot of preparation!

In the same way, you'll want to prepare for your journey into the Bible. The Bible is a wonderful, complex book. Sometimes it's really easy to understand, but other times it will stretch your limits. The journey will take you through the world's creation (Genesis), the battles in ancient Israel (Judges), the miracles of Jesus (Matthew, Mark, Luke, and John), and even the future (Revelation)! How can you prepare for a journey like that?

The best way to prepare is simple: you need to pray.

WHAT IS PRAYER?

Prayer is talking with God. You can pray along with other people or by yourself. You can speak your prayers out loud—shout them, even—or you can whisper like you're telling God a secret. You can even pray silently, knowing that God hears your thoughts (Psalm 139:1-4). No matter how you do it, prayer is a conversation with God.

But conversations are never one-sided. God speaks to you too. One of the ways He does this is through the Bible. Each time you read the Bible, it's best to pray both before and after you read. That way, you start a conversation with God (the prayer before) and then respond to Him (the prayer after).

When you pray, talk with God openly about what you've read in the Bible. Ask Him to help you understand a verse or thank Him for something you discovered. Get into a conversation with your Creator!

God speaks to you through the Bible.

One of the best parts about prayer is that you can pray no matter how you feel—scared, angry, happy, or sad. Feel free to share everything, good or bad, with God. It will help you get closer to Him.

THE UGLY STUFF: SIN, MUDDY PITS, AND DARKNESS

Do you know what *sin* is? A sin is a decision or action that does not please God. It could be anything from stealing or dishonesty to hurtfulness and selfishness. It happens every time we put our desires over God's.

Sin is a muddy pit that traps everyone who falls in. When we get caught in a lie or lash out when someone treats us poorly, we feel stuck inside our own actions.

Everyone is a sinner. The Bible tells us, "All men [and women] have sinned and have missed the shining-greatness of God" (Romans 3:23). Even the nicest, most awesome people you know have sinned. That includes you too.

Don't think that's right? Well, have you ever done something you regretted? Lied to your parents or friends? Stolen a dessert, toy, or dollar bill that wasn't yours? Led someone to believe something that wasn't true?

IMPORTANT PEOPLE

Who Was Paul?

Paul was a Jew whom God used in amazing ways.

When Paul first appears in the Bible, his name is Saul. Saul was a Pharisee from the city of Tarsus. Like many Pharisees, he did not believe that Jesus was the Son of God. In fact, he worked against Jesus' followers by having them imprisoned, beaten, and even killed. If anyone was a sinner, it was Saul. He even called himself "the worst sinner" (1 Timothy 1:15).

While Saul was traveling to a city called Damascus, God appeared to him in the form of a bright light and spoke to him. Saul was blinded for three days, and his life was changed forever. From that day forward Saul—whose name was soon changed to Paul—was a committed follower of Jesus. He traveled widely, starting churches and spreading the good news about Jesus everywhere he went.

God inspired Paul to write letters, which later became books in our New Testament. (We'll learn more about "inspiration" later.) Paul wrote Romans, 1 and 2 Corinthians, Galatians, Ephesians, Philippians, Colossians, 1 and 2 Thessalonians, 1 and 2 Timothy, Titus, and Philemon. You can read about his experience on the road to Damascus—as well as his many other adventures—in the book of Acts.

If you said yes to any of these, that means you've sinned. But you're not alone. Every single person on the planet sins, even the best of us. Just like being stuck in a muddy pit, we can't rescue ourselves. We need someone to pull us out.

God has promised to do this! First John 1:9 says, "If we tell Him our sins, He is faithful and we can depend on Him to forgive us of our sins. He will make our lives clean from all sin." Isn't that awesome? You can't avoid sin on your own. Sooner or later you'll mess up. But God is *faithful*—meaning you can count on Him to never let you down. (More on that word in a later chapter!)

WHY IT'S IMPORTANT TO CONFESS YOUR SINS BEFORE BIBLE STUDY

Imagine exploring a deep, dark cave. You are far underground with a thick rope attached to your belt. On your head is a hard hat with a flashlight strapped to it. You're holding a walkie-talkie in one hand and a small pick in the other. Your archaeologist friends, who are standing far above you in the sunlight, are carefully playing out your rope as you search for long-lost artifacts. But suddenly there's an accident! Your foot slips off a rock and your body slams against the wall, shattering the bulb in your flashlight and knocking the walkie-talkie from your hand. As the deep darkness surrounds you, you realize all communication with your friends has been cut off.

That's what sin is like—a darkness that prevents us from seeing or hearing God. When sin surrounds us, it is impossible to find our way out without help.

That is why the Bible describes Jesus as a light that cannot be overcome by darkness. The Gospel of John says:

Life began by [Jesus]. His Life was the Light for men. The Light shines in the darkness. The darkness has never been able to put out the Light.

JOHN 1:4-5

The best thing to do before reading or studying the Bible is to confess your sin to God. Tell Him all you've done. Don't hide anything. After that, ask for His forgiveness, which Jesus will freely give. Just like shining a spotlight into a pitch-black cave, God will clear up the darkness. Nothing will be in your way to trip you.

Confessing your sin prepares you to get close to God and to hear His voice in the Bible. It's like turning up a microphone. You will hear Him much more

KEY WORDS

Confess and Forgive

Confessing your sin means admitting to God that you have done something that displeases Him. To *forgive* is to excuse or pardon someone who has offended you. You no longer want to pay them back for what they have done.

God forgives us after we confess our sins. See 1 John 1:9.

clearly after the darkness of sin has vanished. Now the real conversation with God can begin. . .and so can our Bible study!

WHAT JESUS SAID ABOUT PRAYER

You can pray loudly or quietly, whenever or wherever you want. But how do you get started? The answer is found in Jesus' teaching.

One day, Jesus spoke to a crowd of hundreds of people, saying:

"This, then, is how you should pray:
'Our Father in heaven, hallowed be your name,
your kingdom come, your will be done,
on earth as it is in heaven.
Give us today our daily bread.
And forgive us our debts,
as we also have forgiven our debtors.
And lead us not into temptation,
but deliver us from the evil one.'"

MATTHEW 6:9–13 NIV

This prayer—which is probably the most famous prayer in the world—is often called "The Lord's Prayer." Let's use it as a model for our own prayers. The best way to practice praying is by imitating Jesus.

HOW TO PRAY LIKE JESUS

First, declare who God is. Jesus began with "Our Father in heaven, hallowed be your name." This identifies God as our Father who lives in heaven. It's like saying, "God, I recognize that You love me and that You are powerful." Jesus also said God's name is "hallowed"—set apart from all other names. It's special and sacred.

Who Wrote the Bible?

The Bible was written by both God and people. Sounds strange, huh? Here's how it happened. God used a process called *divine inspiration* to tell people what to write. It all has to do with God's breath. Seriously!

The book of Genesis records how God created the first humans, a man named Adam and a woman named Eve. It says, "Then the Lord God made man from the dust of the ground. And He breathed into his nose the breath of life. Man became a living being" (2:7). God's *breath* gave Adam life.

God also used His breath to create the Bible. If you look up 2 Timothy 3:16 (we'll learn more about a Bible verse's "address" in a future chapter) it says, "All Scripture is God-breathed and is useful for teaching, rebuking, correcting and training in righteousness" (NIV). God, through His Holy Spirit, breathed on people, "inspiring" them to write the words in the Bible. In other words, the Holy Spirit gave people ideas about what to say. Those people then wrote these ideas down in their own language and style. This is the process of *divine inspiration* and the reason why we say the Bible was written by both God and people.

Who were the people God breathed on? They were many kinds of people, across hundreds of years. Most of them were Jews, who were members of God's chosen nation of Israel. Some were kings (David and Solomon) and others were shepherds (Amos). Luke was a doctor, and Peter and John were fishermen. The book of Psalms—a collection of poems and songs—was written by many authors, some unknown to us today.

We don't know every person God used to write the Bible, but we know many of them. Later in this book you'll learn how to use study Bibles, as well as Bible dictionaries and encyclopedias. These tools will tell you about the author of each book in the Bible.[3]

Lots of people begin with "Dear heavenly Father" or "Dear Lord." Both are respectful and refer to important truths about God. What can you say to begin your prayer?

Second, remember that God is in control. ("Your kingdom come, your will be done, on earth as it is in heaven.") Let God take care of whatever is worrying you. If you are anxious about something, mention it to God. Remember, He controls the whole universe!

Third, share your needs with Him. ("Give us today our daily bread.") Don't be afraid to be totally honest with God. He loves you and wants to hear you speak openly with Him.

Fourth, confess your sin and forgive others. ("And forgive us our debts, as we also have forgiven our debtors.") Remember how sin is like a dark cavern or a muddy pit? It's time to turn on the light and get out the soap. Confess your sin to God. Ask Him to forgive you. And if there is someone you need to forgive, talk with God about that too.

Fifth, ask God to guide you. ("And lead us not into temptation, but deliver us from the evil one.") Living a life that pleases God is not easy. Ask Him for help as you follow Jesus and grow in wisdom.

READY TO EXPLORE!

Archaeologists might need months or even years to prepare for a journey. Fortunately, a few minutes of prayer is all you need for your journey into the Bible. Whenever you pray, you prepare your heart to listen to God's voice through the pages of His Word.

Confessing your sin and asking for forgiveness reminds you of your need for God and His incredible, eternal love for you! He will *always* forgive you! You can always read the Bible with confidence that He loves you and wants to talk with you.

Your prayer time will draw your spirit close to God's Spirit, preparing you to read and study the Bible. Let's go!

TIME TO REVIEW!

Before you read and study the Bible, take time to pray.

- With whom are you talking when you pray?
- Whose "voice" will you hear as you read the Bible?

You sin when you do something that does not please God or that goes against His will. Everyone sins, even the nicest people you know, but God offers forgiveness. Read Romans 3:23 and 6:23.

Jesus taught us how to pray in Matthew 6:9–13. This prayer is often called "The Lord's Prayer." It teaches us to do the following:

- Declare who God is
- Remember God is in control
- Share our needs with Him
- Confess sin and forgive others
- Ask God to guide us

The Bible was written by both God and people through divine inspiration.

CHAPTER THREE

Pack Your Tools
(Resources for Studying the Bible)

*Whatever work you do,
do it with all your heart. Do it
for the Lord and not for men.*
COLOSSIANS 3:23

As an archaeologist, it's your job to dig up important artifacts from the past. Some days you spend in the desert, where it's so hot and dry that your mouth feels like a sandbox. Just below the sand are pieces of ancient pottery, farming tools, cooking utensils, and maybe even the bones of someone who lived centuries ago. On other days you're in a rainy jungle, swatting flies and sloshing through ankle-deep mud. (Good thing you've got boots on!) Underneath the moss and mud lie ancient pyramids, carts, and weapons.

How will you dig up all these amazing artifacts? With *tools!*

To be an archaeologist, you've got to have a bunch of tools. Otherwise, you'll never be able to get the artifacts out of the ground. Archaeologists often use trowels—small, flat spades that are perfect for gently scraping away dirt without damaging the artifact. They also use shovels, brushes, sifters, buckets, and even small metal picks like the ones dentists use to scrape your teeth! (Who knew the ground had cavities?) Each of these tools help archaeologists find the right artifacts and better understand the past.

In the same way, whenever you dig into the Bible, you need to have some tools handy! There are many books, websites, and apps you can use while reading God's Word. Each one is designed to help you dig for God's wisdom. We won't be using any little metal picks (the Bible has no cavities), but these tools are even cooler! Let's look at some of them now.

STUDY BIBLES

When you open a study Bible, you won't just see the 66 books of the Bible. You'll also see short notes, articles, and other bits of information next to the Bible's text. Sort of like a friend writing helpful notes in the margins of a difficult book, study Bibles are meant to help you understand what you're reading.

There are many study Bibles available. Here are a few great ones for kids your age:

- *Dive In! Kids' Study Bible*
- *The Adventure Bible*
- *The Student Bible*
- *Kids' Life Application Study Bible*

JOURNAL AND PEN

Wait a minute! Why would you need a journal and pen? Is this like school? Don't worry, they aren't for homework. They're for writing down what you've discovered in the Bible. Even archaeologists and paleontologists take journals and pens with them on their expeditions. That's how they record the locations of artifacts and dinosaur bones. They may also write down questions for research or plans for their next dig.

As you read the Bible, you will think of important questions too. Write them down in your journal, share

PUT IT INTO PRACTICE

Journaling

Read the story of Daniel and the lions' den in Daniel 6. As you read the story, use your journal to do these things:

☐ Draw a picture of what you think the lions' den looked like.

☐ Write down any words you don't know. You can research them later with some of the tools mentioned in this book.

☐ Try to answer these two questions:
   • Why did some people want to harm Daniel?
   • What was Daniel doing when he was arrested?

☐ List all the incredible things King Darius declares about God at the end of the story.

them with your parents or church leaders, and ask God to help you discover the answers. You can also write down your favorite verses or list the things you read about. (A list of how many times the words "don't be afraid" are used in the Gospels, for example. Or a list of Jesus' miracles.) You can even try to draw the stories you read to help you imagine what they were like. There are lots of good reasons to have a journal and pen with you as you explore the Bible.

BIBLE READING PLANS

A Bible reading plan helps you know which chapter of the Bible to read next. Think of it as a map that archaeologists use to find their way from one site to another. One Bible reading plan might have you read a chapter a day from start to finish. Another might have you spend a month in Matthew or a couple of weeks in Paul's letters. There are many plans out there. Use the ones at the end of this book to get started.

If you don't want to use a plan, you can always read through the Bible book by book, one chapter a day. That's an easy map to follow!

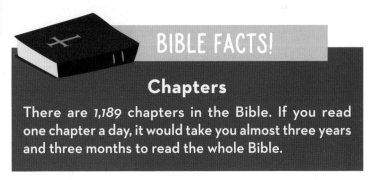

BIBLE FACTS!

Chapters

There are *1,189* chapters in the Bible. If you read one chapter a day, it would take you almost three years and three months to read the whole Bible.

BIBLE DICTIONARIES AND ENCYCLOPEDIAS

These books cover every subject in the Bible from A–Z. (I'm not just saying that. . .they are arranged alphabetically!) You can look up "angels" under A and "Zephaniah" under Z. While regular dictionaries give you a basic definition of each word and show you how to spell it, Bible dictionaries and encyclopedias do much more than that. Each word will have at least a paragraph or two of helpful information.

Ever wondered what the difference is between a Pharisee and a Sadducee? Your Bible dictionary or encyclopedia has you covered! Here are a couple of books to get you started:

- *Discover the Bible: An Illustrated Adventure for Kids*
- *The Student Bible Dictionary, Expanded and Updated Edition* by Johnnie Godwin

CONCORDANCES

A concordance is a book of lists. Some of them list every single time each word in the Bible is used. So if you want to know how often the word *grace* appears in the Bible, just look it up in a concordance. There you'll see a list of every single verse that uses the word. (By the way, *grace* appears 124 times in the NIV.)

Concordances have lots of other features too. For example, since the Bible was originally written in ancient Hebrew, Aramaic, and Greek, many concordances tell which ancient words were translated into the word you are looking up. (The word *grace* is translated from the ancient Greek word *cheris*.)

Many concordances do not have lists for every single word in the Bible. Rather, they include only the words that people are most likely to look up. Other concordances are "exhaustive"—meaning they include every single word in the whole Bible. (These books are huge!)

KEY WORD

Grace

When we receive *grace*—often described as "unmerited favor"—we get something good that we don't deserve.

God has shown us grace in many ways, especially when He sent Jesus, whose sacrifice on the cross paid the cost of our sin.

Biblical Aramaic

Most of the Bible was originally written in ancient Hebrew or Greek. But small portions of the Old Testament, such as the books of Daniel and Ezra, were written in Aramaic. (That's a casual version of Hebrew that was spoken by Jesus and the disciples.) In New Testament times, Aramaic names were often used alongside Greek names. For example, the disciple we call "Peter" (or "Simon Peter") was called *Cephas* by Jesus (John 1:42). *Cephas* is an Aramaic name that means "stone" or "rock."

It's interesting to know that the Bible was originally written in three languages. What's even cooler is the fact that Jesus, even though He is God, talked like a normal, everyday person. This is another way that Jesus shows His love for people—He calls them by name in words they understand.

BIBLE ATLAS

An atlas is a book of maps. Bible atlases provide all kinds of maps of the places mentioned in the Bible. They will help you better understand where these places are located and how far people had to travel to go from one place to another.

For example, do you know where Bethlehem is? You can look it up in a Bible atlas! We often hear about Bethlehem at Christmastime because Mary and Joseph "went up from the town of Nazareth in the country of

Galilee to the town of Bethlehem" (Luke 2:4) before Mary gave birth to Jesus. A Bible atlas shows how far they journeyed and what mountains, rivers, and towns they might have seen along the way.

EPIC STORIES

The Birth of Jesus

You can find the story of Jesus' birth (often called the first Christmas) in two New Testament books. Each book tells different parts of the same story.

Luke 1–2 gives Mary's side of the story. It tells about her cousins Elizabeth and Zechariah, her visit from the angel Gabriel, and the shepherds who visited Jesus.

Matthew 1–2 gives Joseph's side of the story. It includes the wise men's visit from the East and Jesus' escape to Egypt.

In chapter four of this book, we'll talk more about why two books would tell the same story differently.

THE BIBLE ONLINE

There are many websites that can help you study the Bible. Bible Gateway and Bible Hub have helpful articles and multiple translations for free. The website for Our Daily Bread Ministries has free articles, videos, and daily devotions that will help you read the Bible and connect with God every day. For more books like the one you're reading, you can visit the website for

Barbour Books. There are also Bible study groups for kids on social media too.

However, before you visit any websites or social media groups, get permission from your parents—or whoever takes care of you—and let them know which ones you're visiting. There are a lot of great sites out there, but there are some bad ones too.

Talk with your parents—or whoever takes care of you—before you get online. Let them know which sites you are interested in visiting.

Be sure to check out what your church is doing on the internet too. Lots of churches have online activities and Bible studies for kids. Studying the Bible along with your friends at church is really fun!

APPS

Smartphones, tablets, and laptops are everywhere! You probably use them all the time in school. Even archaeologists bring iPads and similar devices with them on their digs. Digital tools can be just as helpful as a trusty trowel.

Just like going on the internet, be sure to check with responsible adults before you download any new apps—even Bible apps. Some Bible apps have Bible dictionaries, atlases, and concordances. Others have Bible studies or Bible reading plans.

New Bible apps are created all the time. Here are a few great ones: YouVersion, Bible App for Kids, LifeWay Kids, and Our Daily Bread.

TIME TO REVIEW!

There are a lot of chapters in the Bible. Do you remember how many?

There are also many tools that will help you explore the Bible. Here are some tools to consider using:

- Study Bibles
- A journal and something to write with
- Bible dictionaries or encyclopedias
- Bible concordances
- Bible atlases
- Bible websites
- Bible apps

The story of Jesus' birth is told in two New Testament books. Which are they?

CHAPTER FOUR

Breaking Ground
(Reading the Bible)

Take hold of teaching. Do not let go.
Watch over her, for she is your life.
PROVERBS 4:13

Get out your trowels and shovels. It's time to go digging!
You can't be an archaeologist or paleontologist without
getting your hands dirty. The only way to find artifacts
and bones is to get down on the ground and dig for them.

One of the most famous archaeological digs happened at Pompeii, a Roman city. In AD 79, the volcano
Mount Vesuvius erupted, burying the whole city in ash
and pumice (a type of glass produced by volcanoes).
Fortunately, this ash and pumice prevented air and
moisture from touching Pompeii's artifacts, so they didn't
break down over time.

When archaeologists dug up Pompeii, they found a
treasure trove of information about ancient Rome! In
fact, much of what we know about ancient Rome comes
from archaeologists' work at this site.

Just like Pompeii's artifacts, the Bible has been

preserved through the centuries for us to study. So grab your shovels! Or in this case, get your pens, notebooks, and highlighters! It's time to dig into God's Word.

HOW THE BIBLE IS ORGANIZED

Imagine opening an app and seeing a colorful menu with 66 different TV shows—all of them related to one another. One show is about the family of a man named Abraham. After that comes a show about the next generation of Abraham's family, then another one about his descendants 300 years later. The next show is a collection of songs and poems written by some of Abraham's descendants, followed by stories about Abraham's great-great-great-(and many more "greats") grandchildren. . . well, you get the point.

This is what the Bible is like. But it's not a collection of shows; it's a collection of books. When you open the Bible, you're opening a library of 66 books (history, poetry, songs, letters, and prophecies) that all tell pieces of one big story—the story of God's love for the world.

These 66 books are divided into two parts—the Old Testament (39 books) and the New Testament (27 books). The time before Jesus' birth is described in the Old Testament, and His birth, life, death, resurrection, and influence on the early church is described in the New Testament.

All books in the Bible—even the ones that are letters—are divided into chapters, and each chapter is broken up into numbered verses.

Who Was Abraham?

When you hear the name Abraham, you might think of President Abraham Lincoln. He's the guy whose face is on the penny and the five-dollar bill. But there's another famous Abraham, this one from the Bible. He was a main character in God's story.

Abraham's original name was Abram. He lived long ago in a land called Ur, and he had a close relationship with God. One day, God made a promise to him that changed the course of history. He said to Abram, "I will make you a great nation. I will bring good to you. I will make your name great, so you will be honored. I will bring good to those who are good to you. And I will curse those who curse you. Good will come to all the families of the earth because of you" (Genesis 12:2–3).

God kept His promise. Abram's descendants eventually became the nation of Israel, often called "God's chosen people." The members of this nation are called Jews (or Israelites). Through His relationship with Israel, God revealed Himself to *all* nations. Hundreds of years after Abraham, Jesus was born as a Jew.

Abraham's story is found in Genesis 12–25, though his name appears throughout the whole Bible. In chapter five of this book you'll learn how to do character studies, which will let you explore Abraham even further!

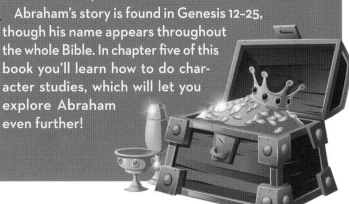

The Bible was not originally divided into chapters and verses. Those were added later to make it easier for people to study the Bible. Think of them as road signs. It's easy to get lost in a big book like the Bible, so the "road signs" help readers know where they are.

The 66 books in the Bible combine to tell God's story. But some of these books are very different from the others. This is because there are many *genres* in the Bible.

PUT IT INTO PRACTICE

Chapters and Verses

Open your Bible to the very first book (Genesis) and find chapter 1, verse 1. Who created everything?

Now use your table of contents to find the book of Psalms. Read chapter 19, verses 1–6. What do these verses say about creation?

You just used the table of contents, the chapters, and the verses in your Bible. Nice work!

WHAT IS "GENRE" AND WHY DOES IT MATTER?

Genre is a cool-sounding word that means "category." (There are a few ways to pronounce this word. Try "JON-rah" for now.) All the books in one genre have similarities. For example, 1 Corinthians and 1 Thessalonians are both letters, so they both have personal greetings in them from the author. However, 1 Kings and 1 Chronicles are both history books, so they each have lots of detailed historical information.

You are already familiar with genres, even if you didn't already know the word. Think of the TV shows you watch. Some shows might be animated, so they are part of the "cartoon" genre. Others might be about games with real-life contestants, so they are in the "game show" genre.

There are many different genres in the Bible—sometimes within the same book! To keep it simple, here's a basic outline of all the Bible's genres.

BOOKS OF THE BIBLE BY GENRE

GENRE	BOOKS OF THE BIBLE
Books of Moses: The first five books of the Bible are very important to the nation of Israel—God's chosen people. These books describe how God created the world, brought the Jews out of slavery, and gave them laws.	Genesis, Exodus, Leviticus, Numbers, Deuteronomy
History Books: These books record how God revealed Himself to His people and guided them into a relationship with Him. One of these books is in the New Testament.	Joshua, Judges, Ruth, 1 and 2 Samuel, 1 and 2 Kings, 1 and 2 Chronicles, Ezra, Nehemiah, Esther, Acts
Books of Prophecy: These books record the words of "prophets"—people whom the Holy Spirit inspired to speak on behalf of God. One of these books is in the New Testament.	Isaiah, Jeremiah, Lamentations, Ezekiel, Daniel, Hosea, Joel, Amos, Obadiah, Jonah, Micah, Nahum, Habakkuk, Zephaniah, Haggai, Zechariah, Malachi, Revelation
Poetic books: These are books of poetry, songs, wise sayings, and stories that teach us how to devote our lives to God, no matter what we're going through.	Job, Psalms, Proverbs, Ecclesiastes, Song of Solomon
The Gospels: These books record the good news of Jesus—His life, teachings, miracles, death, and resurrection.	Matthew, Mark, Luke, John
Letters or *Epistles:* These books are actually letters from early followers of Jesus to other Christians. They show us how to stay close to the Spirit of God.	Romans, 1 and 2 Corinthians, Galatians, Ephesians, Philippians, Colossians, 1 and 2 Thessalonians, 1 and 2 Timothy, Titus, Philemon, Hebrews, James, 1 and 2 Peter, 1 and 2 and 3 John, Jude

WHY DOES IT MATTER WHAT GENRE A BOOK IS?

Knowing the genre of a book helps you read and understand it the right way.

Let's go back to our supercool TV example. Suppose you're about to watch your favorite anime—an awesome style of cartoon that comes from Japan and is filled with action, vibrant characters, and a unique art style.

But let's say you watch an American cartoon like Bugs Bunny instead. If you expect Bugs Bunny to look or feel like anime, you'll be really disappointed! It's an American cartoon with a different pace and style. But if you know what to expect from Bugs Bunny, you'll enjoy it more. The show will mean something different to you because you understand what genre it belongs to.

The same thing is true with genres of the Bible. If you read a history book like 2 Kings and expect it to have stories about Jesus like in the Gospels, you'll be disappointed and miss some important lessons from history. Or if you read a poetic book like Song of Solomon and expect it to have down-to-earth instructions like one of Peter's letters, then you'll miss the whole purpose of the book!

That is why genre matters. When we know what genre we're reading, we can know what to look for. We can think about the ways God might use this unique genre to teach us and reveal something about Himself.

IMPORTANT PEOPLE

Who Was Moses?

Moses was a Jew who was born into slavery in Egypt. However, he was adopted by Pharaoh's daughter and raised alongside Egyptian royalty.

God used Moses to lead the Jews out of Egypt. Then God made Moses their leader as they wandered in the desert on their way to the Promised Land.

Moses wrote the first five books of the Bible, often called "the Books of Moses." These books helped establish the laws and customs of Israel, and they were taught to every Jewish child. Jesus and other Jews in the New Testament would have known the Books of Moses very well.

Moses was *inspired* by the Holy Spirit to write what God wanted. It is likely that Moses also worked with scribes—people who were trained to write and copy books.

Moses is described as a man of great faith.

TIPS FOR READING EACH GENRE

The **Books of Moses** are extremely important to the entire nation of Israel—God's chosen people. He chose to have a unique relationship with them so the world could know and understand Him. When you read these books, pay attention to God's role as the one and only Creator of the universe. Take note of how much He loved the regular, sinful people of Israel (just like He loves you and me). These books are filled with laws, rules, and other important instructions for Israel.

The **historical books** in the Bible are like the history books at school. They are full of stories, battles, government records, and family trees. When you read a historical book, pay attention to the people and the places. Names in the Bible are often full of meaning, so use your Bible study tools to find out what they mean. Ask yourself what you can learn about God from this history.

Prophecy is different from history. Prophets were inspired by the Holy Spirit to speak on God's behalf. Prophets often challenged people to leave their sin and return to God. God used prophets to remind Israel of His covenant with them. When you're reading a book of prophecy, look for these two important things: instructions about worship and instructions about caring for the people in your community.

The **poetic books** are sometimes called "wisdom literature" because they focus on wisdom. In chapter one we learned that wisdom is the ability to make choices that please God. So these books focus on godly living. As you read, remember that they are not going to feel the same as a book of law (like Leviticus) or history books (like 1 and 2 Kings). Poetic books are filled with poetry, songs, and prayers, so they contain lots of figurative language (some call this "word pictures") that helps readers understand important ideas. For example, see if you can find all the images used to describe God!

These books also express a whole range of emotions—sadness, anger, happiness, and even depression—and show us that God welcomes all our questions. We don't need to be afraid to tell Him how we feel.

PUT IT INTO PRACTICE

Images in the Bible

Read Psalm 23. This psalm is about a shepherd. . .*or is it*? Actually, it uses the image of a shepherd to teach us something deeper. Read it again, asking yourself who the "sheep" are and how much God loves them.

We'll learn more about imagery and figurative language in chapter five of this book.

The next genre is the **Gospels**. The word *Gospel* literally means "good news." Each of these books tell about Jesus' life on earth—His teaching, miracles, death, and resurrection. All four Gospels tell one story. But each one focuses on different parts of that story. We'll explore this more in just a minute.

Lastly, there are the **letters**. As you read the letters, pay attention to who is writing and who the audience is. Once you know whom the letter was written to, you can find more about them in your Bible dictionary or Bible encyclopedia. (See chapter three.) Doing this will help you understand the problems the writer was addressing and give you an idea about how to solve similar problems today.

Now, let's take a closer look at one of these genres—the **Gospels**. Let's dig into the four stories of Jesus and see what we can learn. But first, a dinosaur tale.

FOUR STORIES ABOUT THE SAME DINOSAUR

Amy is a paleontologist. Last year she was on a dig and she made a huge discovery—a full stegosaurus skeleton! She dug up the big, beautiful bones with shouts of laughter.

On that day, Amy told about her big discovery in three ways. Later, she told it yet again. All four versions of the story were slightly different, but they were also true.

First, Amy spoke with a news reporter right after finding the bones. She didn't have much time to figure out everything she wanted to say, and the television crew could only give her a few minutes, so she told her story quickly. This version of the story focused on just the basic facts.

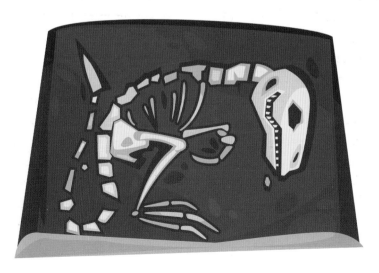

The second time, Amy told the story in epic detail on a video call with her kids. They were wide-eyed as she told them the skeleton was over 20 feet long, had two rows of plates lining its back, and had empty eye sockets just like a dead fish. (Her kids thought that was gross, but also cool at the same time.)

The third time, Amy told the story to her boss, Dr. Bigwig, and the board of directors at the Museum of Science Awesomeness. Her presentation was formal. She used big, official paleontology words like *Jurassic*, *genus*, and *thermoregulation*. This version focused on the science behind the story.

Months after the stegosaurus was assembled, polished, and on display in the Museum of Science Awesomeness, Amy wrote the story again for her blog. This time, she told the story in a brand-new way, explaining the importance of her discovery as a connection to earth's past.

Each version of Amy's story was true. But each one focused on different things for the different people Amy was talking to.

FOUR STORIES ABOUT JESUS

The Gospels—the first four books of the New Testament— are like Amy's four stories about the stegosaurus bones. Each Gospel shares the good news of Jesus' life, death, and resurrection, but they do it in different ways. Each one was written for a different audience.

Matthew, Mark, and Luke were all written around the same time. They all tell the same basic story, but they emphasize different things. . .just like Amy emphasized the facts for the news (Mark), epic details for her kids (Luke), and the big words for her boss (Matthew).

John was written years later. It's very different from the first three Gospels. Sort of like Amy's final story, this Gospel sounds like a friend of Jesus sitting down and reflecting deeply on what the good news really means.

The Gospels can be read by anyone. But each one was originally written to a specific group of people for specific reasons. The table on the next page tells you whom the Gospels were written to. It also shows one big idea and a special name for Jesus that is emphasized in each Gospel. These big ideas reveal why each author chose to write his Gospel.

THE FOUR GOSPELS

	ORIGINAL READERS	ONE BIG IDEA	SPECIAL NAME FOR JESUS
MATTHEW	Jews	Jesus is the "anointed one" who fulfills Jewish prophecies	Messiah
MARK	Romans	Jesus is completely obedient to God	Son of God
LUKE	Greeks (specifically, Theophilus)	Jesus loves every type of person	Son of Man
JOHN	The early church (both Jews and Christians)	Jesus and God are the same	The Word

READING THE BIBLE WITH GENRES IN MIND

No matter what genre of the Bible you're reading, it's important that you pray for God to speak to you. Then listen for His voice as you read. Doing this will help you love Him—and others—more and more as you grow in wisdom!

As you read, remember that the Bible is like a library of 66 different books that come together to tell God's story. The idea that God can speak to us through different genres is amazing! It shows how creative and powerful He is. In the next chapter we'll learn some more ways to study the Bible, and you can combine those with the ones you've just learned. Happy reading!

The Canon of the Bible

Have you ever heard of the biblical *canon*? I know what you're thinking—a big metal barrel with a burning wick on the back and a pile of cannonballs to the side. But that's a *cannon*, not a *canon*.

So, what's a canon? The biblical canon is the collection of 66 books in the Bible. Before the Bible was assembled, the first Christians passed around many other books and letters. But some were not considered to be canon, so they weren't included in the Bible that we have today.

The word *canon* comes from ancient Greek and Hebrew words that literally mean "measuring rod." If a book met certain requirements, it was considered canon and became part of the Bible. If it didn't meet the requirements, it was not included.

WHAT WERE THE REQUIREMENTS?

Early Christians debated each book—especially the New Testament books, which were collected long after the Old Testament books had been decided. They asked these questions:

- *Does the book have divine properties?* In other words, does the book reveal God? Do its claims about God match what the other books reveal? The early Christians carefully examined each book, asking if it taught God's authority, power, beauty, and other qualities. If not, then it was not considered canon.

- *Did the early groups of Christians use the*

books? The Bible includes many stories about the Spirit of God blessing large groups of His followers. While the Spirit certainly blesses individuals, Christianity is clearly meant to be experienced within a loving community. So, when the canon was decided, those in charge of the process paid attention to which books the earliest Christians were using. They trusted the Spirit to guide God's people, just as He had always done.

- *Was the author of the book a prophet, an apostle, or someone very close to a prophet or apostle?* Prophets, such as Jeremiah or Micah, were chosen by God to speak for Him. Apostles, like Peter and John, were eyewitnesses of Jesus' life and work. Paul was considered an apostle because he met Jesus personally on the road to Damascus (Acts 9).

If a book or letter failed to meet all three of these requirements, then it was not included in the Bible.

HOW CAN WE BE SURE THE EARLY CHRISTIANS GOT IT RIGHT?

It's helpful to remember that the early Christians were not *deciding* which books were inspired by God—they were *discovering* them. Just as the Spirit of God inspired people to write the books of the Bible, He also guided the process of collecting those books into one volume. The early Christians did not make these decisions alone—God was actively involved. The Bible is one of God's most important gifts, so we can be confident He got it right.

TIME TO REVIEW!

The Bible is a library of books that tell God's big story. Do you remember how many books there are?

The books of the Bible are divided into different genres:

- The Books of Moses
- History books
- Poetic books
- Books of prophecy
- The Gospels
- Letters (epistles)

There is only one book of prophecy in the New Testament. Do you know which one it is? Compare the list in this chapter with your Bible's table of contents to find out.

The four Gospels tell the same story in different ways. They focus on different big ideas about Jesus. Which Gospel focuses on how Jesus fulfills Jewish prophecies?

BIBLE FACTS!

Mixed Genres

The book of Daniel is a mix of genres. It is part history and part prophecy.

CHAPTER FIVE

Find What You're Looking For (Different Ways to Study the Bible)

*Open my eyes so that I may see
great things from Your Law.*
PSALM 119:18

Have you ever heard of the ancient Mayans? They were a group of people who lived in what is now southern Mexico and the northern part of central America. They made beautiful sculptures, created impressive pyramids, developed advanced farming techniques, and built whole cities.

However, the Mayans died out thousands of years ago. Had it not been for explorers such as John Lloyd Stephens and Frederick Catherwood, we would know nothing about Mayan culture today. Even though Stephens and Catherwood were not the first explorers to discover Mayan ruins and artifacts, they were the first to *record* what they found and share it with others. Stephens was a writer who took lots of notes. Catherwood was an artist who drew detailed pictures. Their work sparked a worldwide interest in the Mayans and inspired many explorers to make their own journeys.[4]

In this chapter we will learn how to study and record what we have found in the Bible, kind of like Stephens and Catherwood's records of the Mayans. But the records you create will change your life.

THREE BIG QUESTIONS ("INDUCTIVE" BIBLE STUDY)

The first way to study the Bible—often called **inductive** Bible study—starts with three big questions, all of which focus on facts and details.

You have probably used a microscope in science class before. By sticking small bugs, bits of plants, or drops of liquid on the glass slides, you can use the microscope's power to view them at extremely close range. Then you simply write down the details of what you saw.[5] Inductive study works a lot like that. You examine small chunks of the Bible, write your observations down, and draw conclusions.

KEY WORD

Inductive

Inductive is a way of thinking (or *reasoning*)—meaning it uses logic to arrive at a conclusion. Inductive Bible study pays close attention to the details of a Bible passage *before* deciding what it means.

Here are the three big questions you'll need to ask for each passage:

1) **Observe**: *What does the passage actually say?*

2) **Interpret**: *What does the passage mean?*

3) **Apply:** *What should I do with what I have learned?*

Let's do a practice run together on Philippians 2:14-15. Start by reading the passage a couple of times:

> *Be glad you can do the things you should be doing. Do all things without arguing and talking about how you wish you did not have to do them. In that way, you can prove yourselves to be without blame. You are God's children and no one can talk against you, even in a sin-loving and sin-sick world. You are to shine as lights among the sinful people of this world.*

After reading the passage, ask yourself, *What does this passage actually say?*

To answer this **observe** question, break it up into six smaller, easier questions: Who? What? When? Where? Why? How?

- *Who?* The book of Philippians was written by the apostle Paul while he was with Timothy. Throughout most of the book, Paul uses the words *I* and *me* to let his readers know he is the main author. At the beginning of the letter, Paul writes, "This letter is to all who belong to Christ Jesus who are living in the city of Philippi and to the church leaders and their helpers also" (1:1). Philippi was a city in Greece.

- *What?* This passage is a command: "Do all things without arguing and talking about how you wish you did not have to do them." It also reminds the Philippians of their true purpose: "You are God's children. . . . You are to shine as lights among the sinful people of this world."

- *When?* The letter doesn't mention a specific time. But a study Bible, a Bible dictionary, or a Bible encyclopedia will tell you Paul wrote this letter within 30 years after Jesus' resurrection.

- *Where?* We know from the *who* question that this letter was sent to the city of Philippi in Greece. The maps in a study Bible or Bible atlas show that Philippi was on the northern edge of the Aegean Sea. Most Bible dictionaries and encyclopedias say that Paul wrote this letter while he was in prison in Rome (Philippians 1:16-24 and Acts 28:11-31).

- *Why?* The answer to this question is found in the first chapter of Philippians: "I pray that your love will grow more and more. I pray that you will have better understanding and be wise in all things" (verse 9). Paul was encouraging the Philippians to love more and live better. He also wanted them to understand that this way of living "come[s] from Jesus Christ, with honor and thanks to God" (verse 11).

- *How?* How were the Philippians supposed to "shine as lights" in a "sin-sick world"? By doing their work gladly and without complaint (2:14).

This attitude would show others in Philippi how joyful life with God can be.

IMPORTANT PEOPLE

Who Was Timothy?

Timothy was a young man who traveled with Paul, helping him plant churches and encourage Christians. (You can read about when he started traveling with Paul in Acts 16:1–5.)

Two New Testament books—1 Timothy and 2 Timothy—are letters (epistles) from Paul to Timothy. These letters were read by many early Christians. In the first letter, Paul tells Timothy how to keep order in the Ephesian church, and he talks about the importance of focusing on the good news of Jesus. In the second letter, Paul passes on more instructions for leading the church. He seems to be handing his ministry over to his young friend.

Now that we have made **observations** about Philippians 2:14-15, it's time to ask the **interpret** question: *What does the passage mean?*

Did you know there are different ways to read the same thing? It's true! Here's an example:

Let's say you and your family sit down together to watch Olympic ice skating. Your sister is watching because she wants to see the beautiful costumes. But your dad is paying close attention to the music, not the costumes. Your mom is ignoring both, focusing instead on how well the skater leaps, spins, and moves. Meanwhile, your younger brother is only watching to find out who wins.

Each person in this example is watching the same competition, but they are each focused on something different. Now let's try reading Philippians 2:14–15 again, focusing on different things this time.

- *Read it literally.* Read the passage a couple of times and focus only on the obvious meaning. Write the words "literal reading" in your journal. Then, after you read, jot down your discoveries underneath. For this passage, you might write something like "Do all things without arguing."

Look Out for Figurative Language!

Remember learning about figurative language in school? Figurative language includes things like similes, metaphors, hyperbole, and other creative ways of speaking. Often, big ideas are easier to understand when we can imagine them as "pictures" in our minds.

The Bible is full of figurative language. In John 15 Jesus calls Himself "the true Vine," with His followers being the "branches." This comparison gave His followers a simple but powerful way to understand their connection with God.

When you read passages literally, watch out for figurative language. Figures of speech help us understand God more deeply, but they shouldn't be taken literally. (For example, Jesus is not literally a vine. He's the Son of God, not a plant!) There is figurative language in Philippians 2:15. Can you spot it?

- *Read it historically.* To answer the "interpret" question, we need to know what the original audience thought about this passage. We can do this by using our Bible dictionaries and encyclopedias. We already know that Philippians was written to Christians in Philippi. What kind of work were they doing? What were they complaining about? When Paul mentioned the "sin-sick world," what kind of sicknesses would they have imagined? Use your Bible study tools to look up Philippi. Then write down whatever information you learn about them.

- *Read it in context.* Read the verses that come before and after the passage you are studying. For Philippians 2:14–15, this might mean verses 12–18, or even the whole chapter. How does your understanding of verses 14 and 15 change when you read them in context?

- *Read to see how they fit together.* Compare this passage to other verses that talk about the same things. Are there other passages that warn against arguing or tell us to shine as lights? Look in the back of your study Bible for a subject index that might show you similar passages. Read each one of these passages. Do they fit together like puzzle pieces? Do they complement each other like matching colors? Write down your answers in your journal.

- *Read it with Jesus in mind.* Following Jesus (believing He is God's Son, receiving forgiveness from God through His sacrifice, and loving others the way He loves) is what makes you a Christian. So looking for references and connections to Him is really important.

Whew! That's a lot! Now that you have all these notes, try to answer the "interpret" question—*what does the passage mean?* Write your answer in your journal.

The last big question in our inductive Bible study is the **apply** question: *What should I do with what I have learned?*

You have just learned so much about Philippians 2:14-15 that you could probably write a paper about it! You know who the author and original audience were, what kind of work Paul's readers probably did, when the letter was written, and even how the verses fit in with the rest of the Bible! You're gaining a lot of knowledge—but remember, your ultimate goal is to know God and grow in wisdom. When we read the Bible, we have to let the Holy Spirit—the Spirit of God—change us.

So how does Philippians 2:14-15 apply to you? Have you learned something about God that makes you want to live differently? Do you think He might be doing something in your life similar to how He worked in the lives of the Philippians? Or have you learned something that makes you want to treat others differently? *What will you do with what you have learned?*

Write down the answers in your journal. God loves you more than you can imagine, and He wants to have a close relationship with you! He wants to talk with you as you pray and read the Bible. He wants to help you love others the way He loves them. He's speaking to you through His Word and through the answers you are writing down. That is what Bible study is all about!

More Passages for Inductive Bible Study

Now that you know how to do an inductive Bible study, try it on your own with the following passages. You will learn so much about God and His love for you!

- Genesis 50:19–21
- Joshua 1:6–9
- Ruth 1:15–18
- Psalm 100
- Proverbs 3:3–8
- Matthew 5:13–16
- Mark 10:13–16
- John 13:1–11
- Colossians 3:15–17
- James 3:1–12

WORD STUDIES

If you were an archaeologist, you would get to learn a bunch of cool new words. *Archaeozoology*, for example, is the study of animal remains—like bones and teeth. Another one is *obsidian*, a black and shiny volcanic rock that can be carved into extremely sharp tools. There's also *excavation*, a word for digging up and recording archaeological sites.[6]

The Bible is full of unique words too. The more you read the Bible, the more you'll find words like *grace*, *mercy*, *holiness*, and *worship*. Doing a **word study** is a great way to figure out what these words mean. Each word in the Bible was carefully chosen by God. Just like a rare artifact gives archaeologists important information about the past, each word in the Bible helps us know God more deeply.

Let's do a word study on the word *faithful*. We'll use the New Life Version of the Bible.

STEP 1: LOOK UP THE WORD

Look up the word in your Bible concordance or go to a website that lets you search the whole Bible. Both tools will list for you every verse that includes the word. Read through the list, picking the verses you want to use for your study.

According to BibleGateway.com, the word *faithful* appears in the New Life Version 263 times—201 in the Old Testament and 62 in the New Testament. That's a lot! We can't study them all in this book. That would take *way* too long. (We'd be as extinct as dinosaurs before we finish.) Instead, we'll look at just these eight verses:

DEUTERONOMY 7:9
"Know then that the Lord your God is God, the faithful God. He keeps His promise and shows His loving-kindness to those who love Him and keep His Laws, even to a thousand family groups in the future."

PSALM 33:4
*For the Word of the Lord is right.
He is faithful in all He does.*

PROVERBS 16:17
*The road of the faithful turns away from sin.
He who watches his way keeps his life.*

DANIEL 6:16
So the king had Daniel brought in and thrown into the place where lions were kept. The king said to Daniel, "May your God, Whom you are faithful to serve, save you."

MATTHEW 25:21
"His owner said to him, 'You have done well. You are a good and faithful servant. You have been faithful over a few things. I will put many things in your care. Come and share my joy.' "

LUKE 16:10
"He that is faithful with little things is faithful with big things also. He that is not honest with little things is not honest with big things."

1 CORINTHIANS 10:13
You have never been tempted to sin in any different way than other people. God is faithful. He will not allow you to be tempted more than you can take. But when you are tempted, He will make a way for you to keep from falling into sin.

1 JOHN 1:9
If we tell Him our sins, He is faithful and we can depend on Him to forgive us of our sins. He will make our lives clean from all sin.

STEP 2: DEFINE THE WORD

Take a look at the verses you've selected. Do any of them explain what the word means?

For example, Deuteronomy 7:9 helps us understand that being faithful means keeping your promises. God is described in this verse as a faithful promise keeper. Luke 16:10 shows us that being faithful means being honest. Also, 1 John 1:9 tells us God will never let us down. We can "depend on Him."

So we can see that faithfulness involves (1) keeping promises, (2) being honest, and (3) not letting people down. Psalm 33:4 plainly describes God as "faithful." That's fantastic news!

After you've written this definition in your journal, you can also look in a Bible dictionary or encyclopedia for more information. But start by doing your own work first. That's the best way to learn!

STEP 3: LOOK AT THE WORD IN ACTION

Look again at the verses you've chosen for the word *faithful*. Do any of them show you solid examples of faithfulness in action?

The answer is yes! Proverbs 16:17 tells us that a faithful person will turn away from sin. In Daniel 6:16, Daniel is thrown into the lions' den as a punishment for being faithful to God. Even though he knew the consequences would be deadly, Daniel still chose to disobey the king's orders not to pray to God. What a faithful guy! In addition, Matthew 25:21 tells of a servant who was rewarded by his boss for his trustworthiness.

So, what does faithfulness look like in action? A faithful person (1) turns away from sin; (2) worships God, not idols; and (3) can be trusted by those in authority (like parents, teachers, coaches, bosses, and God).

First John 1:9 shows how God puts the word *faithful* into action: He forgives us of sin and makes our lives clean. That is how God works in your life and the lives of everyone else who is *faithful* to Him. What could be better than that?

STEP 4: TALK WITH GOD ABOUT THE WORD

Now that you have a definition and examples of the word in action, it's time to pray. Ask God what you should do next. Say something like, "God, now that I know what this word means, what should I do about it? How can I put this word into action? How will this word change my life?"

The answers might come to you right away, or they might come much later. God doesn't promise to answer our prayers immediately. However, God always hears your prayers and is *faithful* to you. (There's that word again!) Psalm 145:18-19 reminds us, "The Lord is near to all who call on Him. . . . He will also hear their cry and will save them."

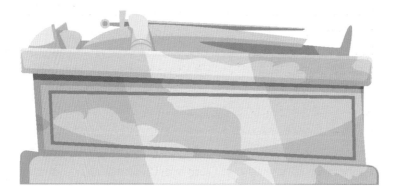

STEP 5: APPLY WHAT YOU'VE LEARNED

It's time to apply the lessons from your word study. In your journal, write down the answers to these questions:

- What will you do differently because of what you have learned?

- How will you follow God right now because of what you have learned about Him?

- Are there small (or big!) things in your life you can change?

- Are there things you need to pray about some more?

Maybe more questions are popping into your head right now. And maybe some of these questions are hard to answer. That's okay! Just like we learned in the inductive Bible study, we grow in wisdom by letting the Spirit of God change us. That might not happen immediately, but we can depend on Him to help us grow.

Other Words Worth Studying

To learn more amazing things about God, as well as how to better love others, try doing a word study on any of these words:

- love
- grace
- sin
- mercy

- peace
- joy
- praise
- forgive

CHARACTER STUDIES

Every great story has memorable characters. Remember Darth Vader from *Star Wars*? Or Ebenezer Scrooge from *A Christmas Carol*? There's also the star detective in the Nancy Drew series and, of course, the mighty lion Aslan from The Chronicles of Narnia. Great characters like these make stories unforgettable. Even bad guys (like Darth Vader) are sometimes needed so that the story can make sense.

The same is true of the Bible. The Bible is one big story—God's story. Each book tells its own story, but they all combine to tell how God created the world, showed His love, and saved us from sin.

God's story is full of interesting characters, such as the hotheaded Peter and the short tax collector named Zacchaeus. There are also Ruth and Naomi—two strong women who faced an uncertain future together—and Esther, the brave and beautiful queen. And don't forget David—that small boy with faith big enough to kill a giant! Whenever we get to know these real-life people the same way we know characters in a story, we will understand the Bible even better.

There are six easy steps for doing a character study. Get out your journal, your pen, and your Bible. You're about to discover a fascinating person!

STEP 1: FIND THE CHARACTER IN THE BIBLE

Look up the character in a Bible concordance, Bible app, or website like BibleGateway.com. These will tell you all the places the character is mentioned in the Bible.

Some characters have the same name—like the Josephs in Genesis and Matthew—so be sure the passages you study are about the same person. Look up that character in a Bible dictionary or encyclopedia if you're not sure.

STEP 2: PRAY, AND THEN READ THAT CHARACTER'S STORY

Ask God to bless your character study. This is important! Tell God the person you are planning to study and ask Him to give you wisdom. After that, read the character's story two or three times. Write down anything interesting you notice. Underline your favorite verses or draw little stars next to them. Read the story until you are familiar with whomever you are studying.

STEP 3: FIND OUT WHERE THAT CHARACTER LIVED

Every story has a setting—the place where the story happens—and every setting affects the story. You can find the setting of a character's story in a Bible dictionary or encyclopedia. You can also find clues in the story itself.

For example, the primary setting of Esther's story is in the Babylonian king's palace. Esther had to follow very specific rules while she was there. Knowing these details will help you understand her story better.

STEP 4: WRITE DOWN THE CHARACTER'S PROBLEMS

Every character in a story faces some kind of problem—or *conflict*. In your journal, write down the conflicts in the story. What problems did your character have to deal with? What made them sad, angry, or scared? There may be just one conflict, or there may be many.

STEP 5: WRITE DOWN WHAT GOD DOES IN THE STORY

Read the story again, this time paying close attention to what God does or doesn't do in the story. Ask and try to answer these questions: *What does this story reveal about God? Is He patient, angry, sad, or something else? Does He act quickly, or does He seem to wait? Does He perform miracles? What kinds of things does He allow? What does He say or do, and why?*

This is how you can learn about God, whether you're studying a character who served Him or a character who did not. Some of the characters in the Bible do almost everything right. . .while others do almost everything wrong! But most of them are just regular people. God's servants often make good *and* bad choices, but God still forgives them.

One of the reasons for studying the Bible is to know this amazingly forgiving God. Character studies are a great place to start!

STEP 6: APPLY WHAT YOU HAVE LEARNED

In this book's introduction, we learned what *apply* means—to take something you've learned and put it to good use. Remember those "apply" questions we asked in the word study? They'll be useful in this study too. Here they are:

- What will you do differently because of what you have learned?
- How will you follow God right now because of what you have learned about Him?
- Are there small (or big!) things in your life you can change?
- Are there things you need to pray about some more?

Now that you know the six steps for doing a character study, let's practice on Samson, an Old Testament character.

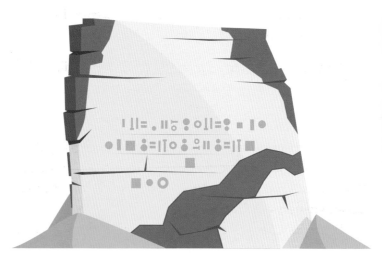

STEP 1: FIND THE CHARACTER IN THE BIBLE

Samson's story is recorded in Judges 13-16. His name is also mentioned in Hebrews 11:32.

STEP 2: PRAY, AND THEN READ THAT CHARACTER'S STORY

Samson's story is rather short, but it has some wild moments! Here are some of the things it includes:

- Samson kills a lion with his bare hands (Judges 14:5-6).

- He makes a bet and tells a riddle (Judges 14:12-14).

- He ties torches to the tails of 300 foxes (Judges 15:4-6).

- He kills 1,000 men with the jawbone of a donkey (Judges 15:13-17).

- His girlfriend, Delilah, tricks him, cuts his hair, and steals his strength (Judges 16:1-22).

- He pulls a house down onto God's enemies (Judges 16:23-30).

You probably didn't know all *this* is in the Bible, did you?

STEP 3: FIND OUT WHERE THAT CHARACTER LIVED

In Samson's time, Israel was not following or obeying God. The people "did evil in the eyes of the LORD" (Judges 13:1 NIV), so God allowed them to be ruled by a ruthless people called the Philistines.

Samson was a Nazirite—someone committed to

serving God in a special way—so he was not allowed to drink wine. Chapter 16 tells us he fell in love with Delilah, a woman who would later help the Philistines capture him. Delilah was from the Valley of Sorek, which means "the valley of vines." It was a place where wine was made. Samson never should have gone there, let alone fallen for a woman there! It was a big mistake—one that eventually led to his death.

STEP 4: WRITE DOWN THE CHARACTER'S PROBLEMS

Samson seemed to have a problem with pride—he thought no one could stop him.

Samson did not seek God's guidance about whom he should marry. His first wife was one of the nation's enemies, a Philistine, and he later spent time with women who made many bad choices. One of them, Delilah, gave him over to the Philistines, who blinded him.

STEP 5: WRITE DOWN WHAT GOD DOES IN THE STORY

At Samson's birth, God told his parents through an angel that Samson would help save the nation of Israel (13:2–5).

Three times in Samson's story, "the Spirit of the Lord" gave Samson supernatural power (13:25; 14:6, 19; 15:14). He was like a real-life superhero!

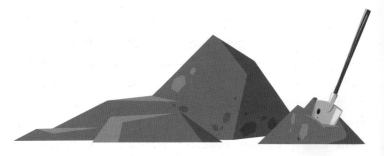

In Samson's final moments, God granted him enough strength to bring down the Philistines' temple. Samson died in the process, but God used this sacrifice to kill His enemies (16:28-30).

STEP 6: APPLY WHAT YOU HAVE LEARNED

To do His work in Israel, God could've picked a humble or patient person. . .but He chose Samson instead. This story shows God can use anyone—even people who struggle to do the right thing—for His mighty purposes. That includes you too!

Samson's life also reminds us how important it is to make decisions that please God rather than ourselves. Imagine how different Samson's life would have been if he had asked God for a godly wife. Instead, Samson behaved selfishly. He spent time with women he was attracted to, not caring whether they followed God. Because he was focused on the wrong things, he eventually lost his eyes—and then his life.

Stay focused on God. Live to please Him first!

DEVOTIONAL READING

Let me tell you the story of a boy named Kevin. Each day, Kevin's mom made him a lunch to take to school and put it in a brown paper bag. On the bag she would write fun, encouraging things. Sometimes it was just "I love you, son." Sometimes it was a funny nickname like "This lunch is for Kevin, the Jedi Master." Or sometimes it was a knock-knock joke. These little notes made Kevin feel close to his mom, even while he was at school. When he got older, his mom would text encouraging

Intriguing Characters in God's Epic Story

Congratulations! Just like an archaeologist digging up mummies (but without all the dust and bones), you've done a character study! Now try studying some of the people in this list. Their stories reveal important things about God and His plans for the world. Learning from their lives will help you grow wiser and closer to God.

- Abram/Abraham
- Joseph (the one in Genesis)
- Hannah
- David
- Ruth
- Esther
- Gideon
- Daniel
- Mary (Jesus' mother)
- Pontius Pilate
- Peter
- John (the disciple)

messages to Kevin. On his birthday, she also sent him funny emails with singing squirrels or dancing puppies. His mom's notes always encouraged Kevin and made him feel close to her. He was never unsure about her love. Even when he was having a bad day, her messages reminded him that she loved him and he could always turn to her for help.

That is what *devotional reading* is like. When we read the Bible like Kevin read his mom's notes, texts, and emails, we open our hearts to a loving relationship with God. Some people call this their "quiet time with God." Other people call it "doing your devotions" or "reading the Bible devotionally." It doesn't really matter what you call it, as long as your heart is open for a relationship with your Creator.

Doing your devotions reminds you of three things:

- Jesus paid for your sin—He *saved* you (1 Peter 2:24).

- You are loved by God and are one of His *children* (Galatians 3:26).

- You are *a new creation* (2 Corinthians 5:17).

It's important to read the Bible every day if you can. (We'll talk more about daily Bible reading in the conclusion.) Setting up a schedule or creating a reading plan is the best way to do this. Just like Kevin's mom, who made a plan and wrote notes for Kevin every day on his lunch bags, these daily readings will make our relationship with God stronger.

What If I Don't Feel Like a New Creation?

Following Jesus and studying the Bible do not mean you will never sin again. You will still make bad choices sometimes. Everyone does—even your grandma, your teacher, and your pastor. Our sinfulness is why we need Jesus.

These are hard things to think about. But there is good news! Your sin doesn't mean you are not part of God's family. You're still a new creation!

The Bible says that your sin is your "old self" trying to come back (Romans 6:6, Colossians 2:11). But if you have decided to follow Jesus, God has made you into a new person. He has saved you from your sins, even the ones you haven't committed yet. You are a *new self*, and God calls you a "new person" and one of His "children" (2 Corinthians 5:17, Galatians 3:26). God says who you are, not your sins!

So when you sin, confess it to God and keep following Jesus. God's love for you will never go away. You may not always feel like you are a new person. Sometimes your "old self" might feel very close. But reading the Bible will remind you that God sees you as someone He has saved and transformed. We could all use that reminder every day!

TIME TO REVIEW!

There are different ways to study the Bible. We've learned about **inductive Bible study**, **word studies**, **character studies**, and **devotional reading**.

Inductive Bible study helps you figure out the meaning of a Bible passage by focusing on the facts and details. You do this by asking the three big questions:

1) Observe: *What does the passage actually say?*

2) Interpret: *What does the passage mean?*

3) Apply: *What should I do with what I have learned?*

Word studies teach you what the unique words in the Bible mean. A five-step process is included in this chapter. Which word would you like to study next?

Character studies show you how people in God's story lived and how God responded to their actions. There is a six-step process included in this chapter. Have you picked a character to study?

Devotional reading happens when you open your heart to a loving relationship with God. It's your "quiet time" with God. In 2 Corinthians 5:17, God calls us a new _____ .

CHAPTER SIX

Save Your Treasure (Making the Bible a Part of Your Life)

Your Word have I hid in my heart,
that I may not sin against You.
PSALM 119:11

Right after an artifact is found, it is first photographed and cataloged. That means the archaeologist will take pictures and measurements, recording as much information as possible. The dig site—the spot where it was found—is also photographed and cataloged. Next, the artifact is cleaned and then packaged for travel. Because artifacts are rare and often delicate, the people who package them wear gloves and are extremely cautious. (Plus, if you were handling a thousand-year-old mummy, you'd want to wear gloves too. Yuck!) To keep them safe on their journey to the museum, the artifacts are wrapped in bubble wrap and packed in large boxes filled with soft material. Once these precious treasures arrive at the museum, even more measures are put in place to keep them safe.

Then there are some treasures that weren't dug up from the ground. In one of the buildings of the National Archives in Washington, DC, are three incredibly important papers: the Declaration of Independence, the Constitution of the United States, and the Bill of Rights. The United States government was (and still is!) built upon these three papers. These documents—which you may have learned about in history class—are treated like treasures. Each one is locked under extremely strong frames of titanium. These frames cost five million dollars and took five years to make![7] The frames protect the papers from thieves and outside air, and the humidity within them is kept at perfect levels. In addition, the papers are placed under thick glass, which is designed to keep out destructive light waves.

When you have such an important treasure, you will do anything to protect it. That's a great way to think about the Bible—as precious treasure! But how can we keep *this* treasure safe in our hearts? By memorizing it and by living it.

DOES THE BIBLE TELL US TO MEMORIZE VERSES?

Earlier, we learned that Deuteronomy is part of the Books of Moses—the first five books of the Bible. These books helped grow the Jews—a group of former slaves wandering in the desert—into a thriving nation. They gave them an understanding of their history, their laws, and their sense of identity. For us, these books are important because they are inspired by God. They reveal both His character and the things He values.

Check out Deuteronomy 6:6-9. This passage says:

"Keep these words in your heart that I am telling you today. Do your best to teach them to your children. Talk about them when you sit in your house and when you walk on the road and when you lie down and when you get up. Tie them as something special to see on your hand and on your forehead. Write them beside the door of your house and on your gates."

Deuteronomy shows how important it is for God's followers to know His Word and apply it to their lives. God expected the Jews to frequently talk about His words as a family. He wanted them to know His Word inside and out.

This same idea pops up throughout the Bible. For example, Proverbs 7:2-3 says, "Keep my words and live. Keep my teachings as you would your own eye. Tie them upon your fingers. Write them upon your heart."

Who wouldn't want to keep their own eyes? If someone offered to trade a million dollars for your eyes, would you accept? No way! You would want to keep them for yourself because they are part of what makes you *you!* That's what memorizing God's Word is like. Once it becomes an important part of you, you'll never want to give it up.

Like the ancient Jews who read the Books of Moses for the first time, you can have a sense of identity by knowing the Bible. It will help you understand what it means to follow Jesus. It pleases God when we take the time to memorize the Bible and make it part of our everyday lives.

WHY DO WE NEED TO MEMORIZE VERSES?

One answer to this question is found in the Psalms: "Your Word have I hid in my heart, that I may not sin against You" (Psalm 119:11).

The writer is telling us that hiding God's Word in our hearts (memorizing it) will help us avoid sin. This is a wonderful way to show God that you love Him. It's similar to obeying your parents. Your mom and dad—or whichever adults you live with—probably *know* that you love them. But when you follow their rules and avoid decisions that make them upset or disappointed, you *show* them your love.

The Gospels of Matthew, Mark, and Luke record a story that shows us the importance of memorizing the Bible. In this story, God's Spirit takes Jesus into the desert alone before Jesus begins teaching and healing people. While He is there, the devil tempts Him three times. But Jesus responds to each temptation by quoting verses from God's Word.[8]

God sees your love for Him in the decisions you

make. Avoiding sin helps you obey the first and greatest commandment: "Love the Lord your God with all your heart and with all your soul and with all your mind" (Matthew 22:37).

EPIC STORIES

Tempted by the Devil

You can find the story of Jesus' temptations in Matthew 4:1–11, Mark 1:12–13, and Luke 4:1–13. Notice how much of the Bible Jesus had memorized. He treasured it!

HOW TO MEMORIZE THE BIBLE

Music: How many of your favorite Disney songs can you sing? How many songs from school, church, family road trips, or Christmastime do you know by heart? The answer to all of these is probably "a lot." That's because music helps us memorize things.

One way to memorize Bible verses is by putting them to music. Lots of musicians have released whole albums of music like this, and you might even sing some of these songs in church.

You can even try to make up the music yourself! It doesn't need to be perfect or even pretty. The music itself isn't the point—it's just a tool to help you write God's Word on your heart and keep it safe, just like a precious treasure.

Rhythm: Another way to memorize words is through rhythm—or pattern in sound. Rhythm is the drumbeat in your favorite song. It's also the reason certain poems are always said the same way.

Here's part of an old nursery rhyme with a strong rhythm. Say it out loud as you read. It will probably sound very familiar.

> *Roses are red.*
> *Violets are blue.*
> *Honey is sweet.*
> *And so are you.*

PUT IT INTO PRACTICE

Rhythm

Here are two verses with strong natural rhythms. Try saying them out loud a few times. Picture a drummer in a marching band, keeping a beat. DUM. da-DUM. DUM. da-DUM. Exaggerate the sounds in each line. See if you can hear their natural rhythms.

ROMANS 6:23 KJV

For the wages of sin is death;
but the gift of God
is eternal life
through Jesus Christ our Lord.

1 PETER 5:7

Give all your worries to Him
because He cares for you.

It's easy to memorize this poem because its pattern of sounds—its rhythm—is so strong.

Now try taking your favorite Bible verse and putting it to a rhythm. You can either make up your own rhythm or use the natural rhythm of the words themselves. Say the verse over and over in the same way, using the same rhythm each time. The rhythm will eventually come naturally to you, making it easy for you to remember the words.

Flash Cards: Another way to memorize the Bible is to use flash cards. Flash cards are small pieces of paper with the verse or part of the verse written on them. When you use flash cards, you look at just one card at a time. That way, your brain actively focuses on one thing, making memorization much simpler.[9] It's like a workout for your mind!

PUT IT INTO PRACTICE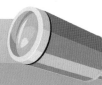

Flash Cards

Try putting each of these lines on the front and back of flash cards. You will need six cards. Look at the front of the first one and say it out loud. Then try to say what's written on the back. Don't turn the card over until you've said the next line, then flip it over to see if you were correct. If not, say what is written on the back side and start again. If you do this over and over for each card, pretty soon you'll have two new verses memorized!

Romans 10:9–10

Card 1, Side 1: *If you say with your mouth*
Card 1, Side 2: *that Jesus is Lord,*

Card 2, Side 1: *and believe in your heart*
Card 2, Side 2: *that God raised Him from the dead,*

Card 3, Side 1: *you will be saved*
Card 3, Side 2: *from the punishment of sin.*

Card 4, Side 1: *When we believe in our hearts,*
Card 4, Side 2: *we are made right with God.*

Card 5, Side 1: *We tell with our mouth*
Card 5, Side 2: *how we were saved*

Card 6, Side 1: *from the punishment of sin.*
Card 6, Side 2: *Romans 10:9–10*

Write It Down: Another way to memorize the Bible is by writing it down. Once you've picked a verse or two to memorize, write it on a blank sheet of paper. Then do it again. And again. And again, and again, and again. You can memorize almost anything if you repeat it enough!

Do you have some spare time on your morning bus ride to school? How about while you're eating breakfast? Or maybe before bed? Just like using flash cards, writing down a passage to memorize is a good workout for your brain. So pull out your journal right now, and let's get started!

Be sure to compare the original passage in the Bible to what you've written, just to make sure you've got it right. Before long you'll have the treasure of God's Word written on your heart.

Write It Down

Try an experiment this week. Pick one of the verses below and write it in your journal two times before school and three times before bed. Do this each day, Monday through Friday. That's a total of 25 times after the week is over. At the end of the week, see if you have memorized the verse. You might surprise yourself!

- Galatians 5:22-23
- Proverbs 3:5-6
- Joshua 1:9
- Isaiah 40:31

LIVE WHAT YOU'VE LEARNED

Let's imagine a young girl—we'll call her Stacey—whose favorite Disney movie is *Frozen*. Stacey *loves* to sing that movie's songs. She knows every line, every scene, and every dance move. She even changes her voice to sound like the characters. You probably know someone just like this, don't you? Or maybe that person is you!

The point is that Stacey loves these songs so much that she *lives* them. It's not enough for Stacey to sing "Let It Go" while just sitting still. She needs to pretend she's Elsa while she's doing it! She wants to live what she has learned.

That's the whole point of memorizing the Bible too. Archaeologists don't ship their artifacts back to the museum only to keep them locked in the basement. They put them on display for all to see!

God doesn't want us to hide the treasures we've

discovered in His Word as a secret. He wants us to share them with everyone! So, if you've memorized a verse like Ephesians 4:32—which tells us to forgive and be kind to each other—then put it into practice!

Or, if you've memorized a verse like Joshua 1:9—which tells us to have strength of heart because God is always with us—then pray about whatever makes you afraid.

As you explore the Bible, you'll dig up some amazing treasures. God will speak to you through what you read, and you'll find encouragement and hope. Memorizing what you've read is a wonderful way to keep these treasures nearby. But don't stop there. Live what you've learned!

Why Are There Different Versions of the Bible?

You may have already noticed that there is more than one version of the Bible. In fact, there are hundreds. They have names like New Life Version (that's the version most often used in this book), New International Version, King James Version, or English Standard Version. Often, there's an abbreviation of the version after the chapter and verse numbers.

For example, here are four different versions of Psalm 100:1.

Call out with joy to the Lord, all the earth.
(Psalm 100:1 NLV)

Shout for joy to the LORD, all the earth.
(Psalm 100:1 NIV)

Make a joyful noise to the LORD, all the earth!
(Psalm 100:1 ESV)

Make a joyful noise unto the LORD, all ye lands. (Psalm 100:1 KJV)

Look at all the differences! The English Standard Version (ESV) uses an exclamation point while the others use a period. The King James Version (KJV) uses the old word "ye" (we would say "you" today). The New International Version (NIV) says to "shout," and the New Life Version (NLV) says to "call." The other two say, "Make a joyful noise." You can probably spot more differences yourself. The words are different in each version, yet they all have the same meaning. But why? Shouldn't all versions of the Bible be exactly the same?

We learned earlier that the Bible was originally written in ancient Hebrew and Greek (with a few passages in Aramaic). So the Bible must be *translated* into modern English in order for you to read it. There are a lot of differences between languages, especially between ancient and modern ones. Sometimes, a phrase or idea in one language doesn't even exist in the other. Other times, a word in one language could mean many things in another. That's how we get the words "shout," "call," and "make a noise" from the same ancient Hebrew word in Psalm 100:1.

Here's an example of how tricky it can be. Imagine you are eating lunch with two friends in the school cafeteria. A third friend named Rafael sits down. Rafael, who speaks Spanish, says to everyone, "Hola, mis amigos!" Your Spanish teacher walks over and asks you and your other two friends to write down in English what Rafael said.

You write, "Hey, guys!"

One of the others writes, "Hi, dudes!"

Your second friend writes, "Hello, my friends!"

Did Rafael say hey, hi, or hello? Did he call the group

guys, dudes, or friends? Who wrote the right translation?

All of you did! Depending on the situation, any of those three English sentences can be used to express the same thing. To figure out exactly which one Rafael meant, the teacher would have to ask him directly. When scholars translate the Bible from ancient languages, they can't ask the original authors what they meant. (Because they're all long gone!) That's why translation is so hard.

But you don't need to worry about Bible translations—leave that to the experts! All the major translations are trustworthy. Whenever you're studying a Bible passage, read it in multiple translations to understand different parts of the passage. But when you're reading the Bible as part of your "quiet time," find a translation that's easy for you to understand. (Try the New Life Version, the New International Version, or the New Living Translation.) Or, if your parents or church has a favorite translation, start with that one.

Now you know what those letters at the end of verse references are! How many different translations have you seen in this book?[10]

TIME TO REVIEW!

It's important to memorize our favorite verses from the Bible. According to Proverbs 7:2-3, what do Bible verses contain and where should we write them?

Memorizing the Bible will remind you that you are a child of God. It will also help you avoid _____.

Jesus demonstrated the power of God's words when He was tempted by the devil (Matthew 4:1-11).

You learned four different ways to memorize the Bible:

- *Music*: sing the verse as a song.

- *Rhythm*: focus on the patterns of sound in the words, and keep repeating that pattern.

- *Flash cards*: use cards to give your brain a workout.

- *Write it down*: write down the passage many times each day.

There are many different translations of the Bible. Find one that is easy for you to understand—such as the New Life Version—and read it.

We memorize the Bible so we can live what we have learned. Jesus taught us to love God and love others. Memorizing the Bible helps us do both!

CONCLUSION

Keep Digging! Keep Exploring!

The Good News tells us we are made right with God by faith in Him. Then, by faith we live that new life through Him. The Holy Writings say, "A man right with God lives by faith."

ROMANS 1:17

This is your official invitation to a life full of adventure! The steamboat to the Amazon rain forest is getting ready to move! The caravan into the African countryside is rolling out! The deep dig into God's Word is about to begin!

As you study the Bible and put what you've learned into practice, you will grow in your understanding of God as your Creator and Friend. Then you will see Him do amazing things in your life and in the lives of others.

So what are you waiting for? Let's go dig up some truth!

DAILY BIBLE READING

Reading the Bible every day will make your relationship

with God stronger—something that God truly desires. Just like family relationships, your relationship with God will grow weaker if you don't talk with Him very much. In chapter five you learned how to have a "quiet time with God" by reading the Bible devotionally. The best way to do this, you learned, is to set a schedule and stick to a daily routine.

So what Bible reading schedule works for you? Could you schedule time in the morning before school to read one chapter every day? What about at bedtime? After you've changed into your pajamas and brushed your teeth, you could read a little bit of the Bible before you sleep. Or maybe your family would like to read parts of the Bible together at dinnertime? If a whole chapter is too much, try reading just ten verses at a time.

Where or how much you read isn't important. What's important is that you make a plan for Bible reading and try to stick to it.

If you miss days here and there, don't worry. God is not an angry teacher with a red pen. Reading the Bible every day is not a test or a chore. It's a *gift*. As your Father, God loves you very much, and He has revealed Himself and His wisdom through the Bible. So when you read it, you're having a conversation with Him. It's the perfect way to draw close to your heavenly Father.

Reading the Bible every day is a gift. It's a conversation with God, who loves you very much.

BIBLE READING PLANS

So, now you're ready to read the Bible! There are lots of ways to get started. Sometimes it's helpful to have a checklist—a Bible reading plan—so you know what to read next. Here are a few to get you going!

THE STORY OF JESUS IN ONE MONTH

Do you want to read Jesus' full story? Try this reading plan. It will take you into each Gospel. You'll read about Jesus' teachings, His miracles, His parables, His death on the cross, His resurrection from the dead, and more!

- Day 1: Matthew 1:18–24
- Day 2: Matthew 2:1–12
- Day 3: Luke 1:5–25
- Day 4: Luke 1:26–56
- Day 5: Luke 1:57–80
- Day 6: Luke 2:1–20
- Day 7: Luke 2:41–52
- Day 8: John 1:1–14
- Day 9: Mark 1:1–20
- Day 10: John 2
- Day 11: Matthew 5
- Day 12: Matthew 6
- Day 13: Matthew 7
- Day 14: Mark 4:1–34

- Day 15: Mark 6:30–44
- Day 16: Mark 6:45–56
- Day 17: Luke 15:1–10
- Day 18: Luke 15:11–31
- Day 19: Mark 10:13–31
- Day 20: Matthew 22:34–40
- Day 21: Luke 19:1–10
- Day 22: Luke 9:28–36
- Day 23: Mark 11:1–11
- Day 24: John 15:1–17
- Day 25: John 19:1–27
- Day 26: John 19:28–42
- Day 27: John 20:1–18
- Day 28: John 20:19–31
- Day 29: John 21
- Day 30: Matthew 28:16–20; Acts 1:1–11

TWO WEEKS OF JESUS' MIRACLES

We know Jesus is God's Son because of the many miracles He performed. As you read each of these, think about God's incredible power and love for everyone. . . including you!

- Day 1: John 2:1-11 (Water into Wine)
- Day 2: Matthew 8:1-4 (Man with Leprosy)
- Day 3: Mark 5:1-20 (Demon-Possessed Man)
- Day 4: Luke 8:41-56 (Dead Girl and Sick Woman)
- Day 5: John 5:1-15 (Healing at the Pool)
- Day 6: Luke 9:10-17 (Feeding 5,000 People)
- Day 7: Matthew 14:22-33 (Walking on Water)
- Day 8: John 9:1-12 (The Man Born Blind)
- Day 9: John 11:1-44 (Lazarus)
- Day 10: Mark 9:2-8 (The Transfiguration)
- Day 11: Luke 9:37-42 (The Boy with an Evil Spirit)
- Day 12: Mark 10:46-52 (Blind Bartimaeus)
- Day 13: Luke 24:1-10 (Jesus Rises from the Dead)
- Day 14: John 21:1-7 (Miraculous Catch of Fish)

TWO WEEKS OF JESUS' PARABLES

One of the reasons Jesus' teachings are so memorable is because He taught in *parables*—short stories that use ordinary things to explain spiritual truths. Each parable has a main idea. As you read each one, ask yourself, "What's the point of this story?" And then, "How will I respond?"

- Day 1: Mark 4:21-25 (The Lamp)
- Day 2: Mark 3:23-27 (The Divided Kingdom)
- Day 3: Mark 4:26-29 (The Growing Seed)
- Day 4: Matthew 13:31-32 (The Mustard Seed)
- Day 5: Matthew 13:44 (The Hidden Treasure)
- Day 6: Luke 10:29-37 (The Good Samaritan)
- Day 7: Luke 11:5-13 (The Friend at Midnight)
- Day 8: Matthew 18:10-14 (The Lost Sheep)
- Day 9: Luke 15:8-10 (The Lost Coin)
- Day 10: Luke 15:11-32 (The Lost Son)
- Day 11: Matthew 18:23-35
  (The Unforgiving Servant)
- Day 12: Matthew 25:14-30
  (Ten Talents or Gold Coins)
- Day 13: Luke 18:9-14
  (The Pharisee and the Tax Collector)
- Day 14: Mark 13:28-37
  (The Fig Tree and the Servant at the Door)

TWO WEEKS WITH AMAZING WOMEN IN THE BIBLE

Young girls today face unique challenges, and the world's expectations for them can feel overwhelming! However, some of the Bible's best stories feature women and girls who were used by God to overcome enormous challenges. If you are a girl, remember that God loves you exactly the way you are! You are His precious, beautiful daughter. If you're a boy, thank God for the amazing women in your life and in the Bible.

- Day 1: Ruth 1 (Naomi and Ruth)
- Day 2: Ruth 2 (Ruth Meets Boaz)
- Day 3: Ruth 4:13-22 (Ruth in the Line of David)
- Day 4: Judges 4 (Deborah and Jael)
- Day 5: 1 Samuel 1 (Hannah's Sacrifice)
- Day 6: 1 Samuel 2:1-11 (Hannah's Prayer)
- Day 7: Esther 2 (Esther Made Queen)
- Day 8: Esther 7 (Esther's Brave Request)
- Day 9: Esther 9:1-17 (God's People Triumph)
- Day 10: Proverbs 4:1-9; 8:1-11 (Wisdom Described as a Woman)
- Day 11: Proverbs 31:10-31 (The Noble Woman)
- Day 12: Luke 1:26-38 (Mary's Faith and Trust)
- Day 13: Luke 1:46-56 (Mary's Powerful Song)
- Day 14: John 12:1-8 (Jesus Anointed by a Woman)

TWO WEEKS IN THE PSALMS

You learned in chapter four that Psalms is a poetic book. It is a collection of songs, prayers, and poems. In each psalm, the author expresses his joy and sadness to God without fear or shame. Psalms also contains some of the most beautiful images of God and His creation. Try including verses from your favorite psalms in your prayers each day. Use them as a way of telling God what's on your heart.

- Day 1: Psalm 1
- Day 2: Psalm 13
- Day 3: Psalm 15
- Day 4: Psalm 19
- Day 5: Psalm 23
- Day 6: Psalm 40
- Day 7: Psalm 67
- Day 8: Psalm 84
- Day 9: Psalm 100
- Day 10: Psalm 119:1–16
- Day 11: Psalm 119:97–112
- Day 12: Psalm 121
- Day 13: Psalm 136
- Day 14: Psalm 150

TWO WEEKS IN THE PROVERBS

Earlier in this book, you saw that Proverbs is also a poetic book, offering wise sayings to help us live godly lives. The writers of Proverbs, including the wise King Solomon, made a bunch of short, thought-provoking statements that are designed to help us learn truth. Many times, the writers would state a truth and then its opposite, to help you understand wisdom from every angle. (Here's an interesting note: Proverbs has 31 chapters, just like many months have 31 days. A lot of people read through the book of Proverbs every month!)

- Day 1: Proverbs 1:1–9
- Day 2: Proverbs 3:1–7
- Day 3: Proverbs 6:6–11
- Day 4: Proverbs 8:1–10
- Day 5: Proverbs 11:1–4
- Day 6: Proverbs 12:1–7
- Day 7: Proverbs 14:34–35
- Day 8: Proverbs 16:2–7
- Day 9: Proverbs 17:27–28
- Day 10: Proverbs 19:16–17
- Day 11: Proverbs 22:1–4
- Day 12: Proverbs 21:21–23
- Day 13: Proverbs 24:1–5
- Day 14: Proverbs 27:1–2

- Day 1: Genesis 37; Acts 7:9
  (Envy Destroys Relationships)

- Day 2: Exodus 33:8–23; James 2:23
  (The Friend of God)

- Day 3: Leviticus 19:16–18; Matthew 22:34–40
  (Loving Your Neighbor)

- Day 4: Deuteronomy 13:1–8
  (Beware of the Influence of Friends)

- Day 5: Psalm 109 (Deceit Destroys Relationships)

- Day 6: Proverbs 12 (Listening to Wise Advice)

- Day 7: Proverbs 15:17–18; 22:24–25
  (Anger Destroys Relationships)

- Day 8: Proverbs 16:27–28
  (Gossip Destroys Relationships)

- Day 9: Proverbs 18:24 (Being a Friend)

- Day 10: Proverbs 27:5–11; Ephesians 4:14–29
  (Speaking the Truth in Love)

- Day 11: Ecclesiastes 4:9–12; Daniel 1
  (Strength in Numbers)

- Day 12: Luke 15 (Rejoicing Together)

- Day 13: Romans 14:13–23 (Working toward Peace)

- Day 14: Hebrews 13:1–3; 1 John 2:1–14
  (Brotherly Love)

TWO WEEKS TO GROW IN FAITH

- Day 1: Genesis 22:1-14
  (Trusting God with Everything)
- Day 2: 1 Samuel 1:7-20
  (Trusting God through Prayer)
- Day 3: 2 Chronicles 20:20-30
  (Trusting God for Protection)
- Day 4: Daniel 3 (Trusting God to the End)
- Day 5: Isaiah 40:27-31; Mark 10:13-16 (Faith Grows)
- Day 6: Hebrews 4:16; 10:19-25
  (Faith to Approach God)
- Day 7: 1 John 2:3-6; 2 John 6-9
  (Obedience to His Commandments)
- Day 8: 1 Samuel 15:12-23
  (Obedience Is Better Than Sacrifice)
- Day 9: Luke 6:46-49; Acts 4:18-21
  (Obedience Brings Strength)
- Day 10: Psalm 1: Acts 5:28-32 (Obedience to Truth)
- Day 11: Genesis 12:1-4; Deuteronomy 11:1-15
  (Obedience without Question)
- Day 12: Leviticus 26:1-13; Psalm 119:56-62
  (Obedience Brings Blessing)
- Day 13: Jeremiah 11:3-5; 2 Peter 1:3-8
  (Growth through His Promises)
- Day 14: Ephesians 5:1; Philippians 1:27; 1 Peter
  1:13-22 (Growth through His Likeness)

TWO WEEKS TO BETTER CHOICES

- Day 1: Matthew 6:25–34 (Seek God First)
- Day 2: Luke 6:3; Philippians 2:3–4 (Put Others' Needs First)
- Day 3: Proverbs 19:11 (Try Not to Be Offended)
- Day 4: Proverbs 15:1–2; 16:24; 18:21 (Think Before You Speak)
- Day 5: James 1:2–4 (Choose Joy)
- Day 6: Proverbs 10:4–5; 18:9 (Work Hard)
- Day 7: Matthew 6:21; 1 Timothy 6:10 (Beware the Love of Money)
- Day 8: Proverbs 3:11–12 (Accept Correction)
- Day 9: Proverbs 23:7; Philippians 4:8 (Guard Your Thoughts)
- Day 10: Proverbs 2:6; James 1:5–8 (Ask God for Wisdom)
- Day 11: 1 Thessalonians 5:16–18 (Pray, a Lot!)
- Day 12: Joshua 1:8; Psalm 1:1–3 (Think about God's Word)
- Day 13: 1 Peter 2:13–17 (Follow the Rules That Follow God's Rules)
- Day 14: 2 Chronicles 7:14; Proverbs 22:4 (Be Humble)

*How can a young person stay
on the path of purity?
By living according to your word.
I seek you with all my heart;
do not let me stray from
your commands.*

PSALM 119:9–10 NIV

GLOSSARY

canon: the Bible's 66 books that early Christians agreed were inspired by God.

confess: telling God you have sinned; admitting that you have done something that displeases Him.

covenant: a binding promise made between God and man. It requires faithfulness on both sides.

divine inspiration: the process God used to write the Bible. He breathed on various people, giving them His idea of what to write. Then those people wrote these ideas down in their own language and style.

epistle: a letter; a genre of scripture. Twenty-one New Testament books are epistles.

faith: Hebrews 11:1 describes faith as "being sure we will get what we hope for" and "being sure of what we cannot see." God is very pleased when people have faith in Him. Ephesians 2:8–9 tells us that we are saved from our sins by grace "through faith" in Jesus' sacrifice.

forgive/forgiveness: to excuse or pardon someone who has offended you. You no longer want to pay them back for what they have done.

Gospel: the good news that Jesus has paid the cost of our sin and saved us from separation from God. People who believe Jesus is God's Son and trust in Him for the forgiveness of their sins will spend eternity with God. See Ephesians 2:1–8. This word can also refer to a genre of scripture or one of the four books that record Jesus' life on earth—Matthew, Mark, Luke, and John.

grace: unmerited favor; receiving something good that you don't deserve.

incarnate: "in the flesh." Jesus is God incarnate. He is fully God and fully human.

Messiah: means "anointed one" in Hebrew. God promised to send the Messiah as a descendant of King David, and Jesus fulfilled the prophecy. In Greek, the word is *christos*, which is where we get the title "Christ" for Jesus.

reveal: how God makes Himself known. The Bible reveals how God acts, what He thinks and says, and what He values.

scripture: the books of the Bible; a passage from the Bible.

sin: a decision or action that does not please God or goes against His will.

Son of God: a name for Jesus. "We know God's Son has come. . . . We are joined together with the true God through His Son, Jesus Christ. He is the true God and the life that lasts forever" (1 John 5:20).

Son of Man: one of the ways Jesus described Himself. The phrase is taken from Daniel 7:13-14: "I kept looking in the night dream and saw One like a Son of Man coming with the clouds of heaven. . . . All the people of every nation and language would serve Him. His rule lasts forever. It will never pass away. And His nation will never be destroyed."

triune: three in one. God is three separate persons in one God—God the Father, God the Son (Jesus), and God the Holy Spirit.

NOTES FOR
BIBLE EXPLORERS

[1] You can read all about these awesome commandments in Matthew 22:34–40.

[2] Gordon D. Fee and Douglas Stuart, *How to Read the Bible for All It's Worth,* Third Edition (Zondervan, 2003), 225.

[3] These ideas can be found in the *Dive In! Kids' Study Bible: New Life Version* (Barbour Publishing, Inc., 2020).

[4] "Early Explorers of the Maya Civilization: John Lloyd Stephens and Frederick Catherwood," Joshua J. Mark, https://www.ancient.eu/article/419/early-explorers-of-the-maya-civilization-john-lloy/ Accessed 10/27/20.

[5] Try comparing iodized salt and sea salt under a microscope sometime. You can probably find both in your kitchen. They taste the same on food, but a microscope will reveal many differences in shape, size, and color.

6 These definitions are adapted from the online glossary of the Archaeological Institute of America. https://www.archaeological.org/programs/educators/introduction-to-archaeology/glossary/. Accessed 10/14/20. https://museum.archives.gov/founding-documents. Accessed 10/24/20.

7 https://www.popularmechanics.com/technology/security/a15895554/how-to-protect-the-declaration-of-independence/. Accessed 10/24/20.

8 Jesus quotes Deuteronomy 8:3, 6:16, and 6:13.

9 https://www.brainscape.com/blog/2011/04/reasons-why-flashcards-are-so-effective/. Accessed 10/23/20.

10 There have been four: the New Life Version, New International Version, King James Version, and English Standard Version.

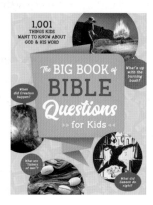